Guide to Wildlife Watching
in Oregon

Grant McOmie

WESTWINDS
PRESS®

Library of Congress Cataloging-in-Publication Data

McOmie, Grant.
  Grant's getaways : guide to wildlife watching in Oregon / Grant McOmie.
    pages cm
  Includes index.
  ISBN 978-1-941821-47-3 (pbk.)
  ISBN 978-1-941821-75-6 (e-book)
  ISBN 978-1-941821-83-1 (hardbound)
  1. Wildlife watching—Oregon—Guidebooks. 2. Oregon—Guidebooks. I. Title.
QL201.M36 2015
590.72'34795—dc23
                                    2015003675

Edited by Michelle Blair
Designed by Vicki Knapton
Map by Gray Mouse Graphics and Vicki Knapton

Published by WestWinds Press®
An imprint of Turner Publishing Company
4507 Charlotte Avenue, Suite 100
Nashville, TN 37209
(615) 255-2665
www.turnerbookstore.com

For Steve Medley—and the long-ago travels and wildlife
adventures that we shared—
they forever changed my course in life.

And

For my wife—Christine—my finest and favorite travel
companion and the part of my life that I call happiness.

Contents

Fall Grant McOmie's Outdoor Talk—Bullets and Greed 113

October

November

December

Winter Grant McOmie's Outdoor Talk—
A Walk on the Wild and Woolly Side of Oregon 153

January

February

March

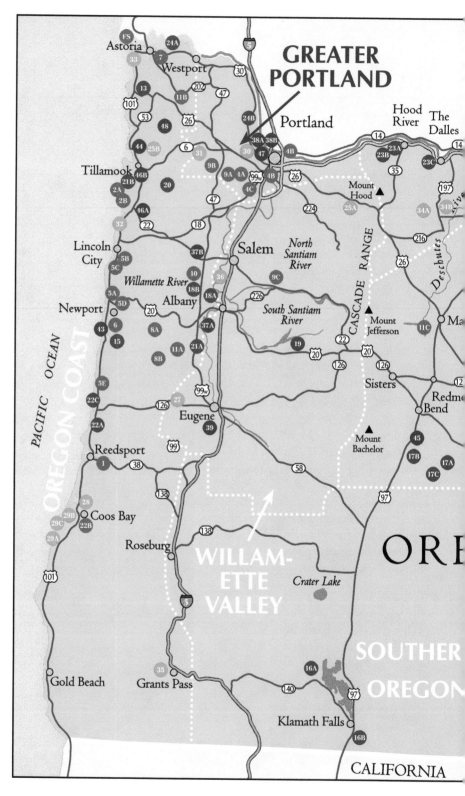

GREATER
PORTLAND

Astoria
FS
33
7
24A
Westport
30
13
11B
202
47
101
53
26
24B
Portland
Hood
River
The
Dalles
48
38A 38B
14
Tillamook
44 25B
6
31
30
47
4B
23A
23B
23C
14
9B
9A 4A
99w 4B
26
35
197
46B
21B
20
4C
224
Mount
Hood
2A
2B
47
25A
34A
34B
16A
22
18
Lincoln
City
5B
37B
Salem
North
Santiam
River
216
26
CASCADE RANGE
Deschutes
5C
Willamette River
10
36
9C
Newport
5A
5D
18B
Albany
18A
226
South Santiam
River
Mount
Jefferson
11C
Ma
43
6
20
8A
37A
22
20
15
11A
21A
19
20
126
126
8B
Sisters
12
PACIFIC OCEAN
OREGON COAST
5E
99w
Redm
Bend
22C
126
27
Eugene
22A
99
39
Mount
Bachelor
45
17B
17A
Reedsport
1
38
17C
58
97
138
28
29B
Coos Bay
29C
22B
O R E
29A
138
Roseburg
WILLAM-
ETTE
101
Crater Lake
VALLEY
5
35
16A
SOUTHER
Gold Beach
Grants Pass
140
97
OREGON
Klamath Falls
16B
CALIFORNIA

6

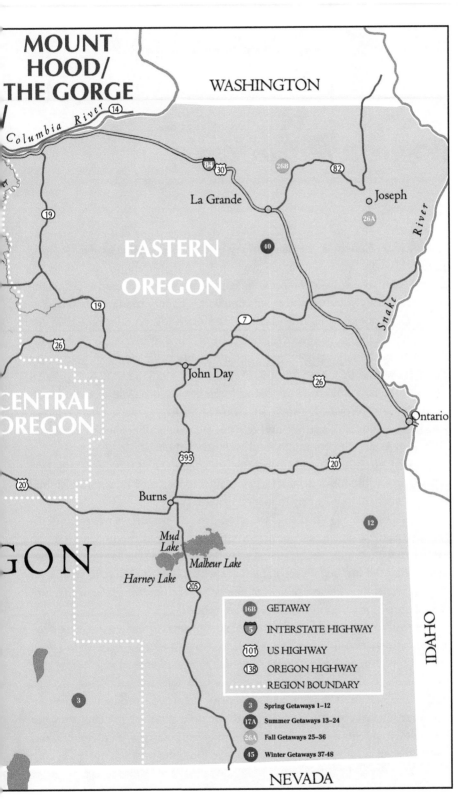

MOUNT HOOD/ THE GORGE

WASHINGTON

Columbia River 14

84 30

26B

82

La Grande

Joseph

26A

19

EASTERN

OREGON

19

40

River

7

Snake

26

26

John Day

CENTRAL
OREGON

Ontario

395

20

20

Burns

12

Mud
Lake

Malheur Lake

GON

Harney Lake

205

3

16B	GETAWAY
5	INTERSTATE HIGHWAY
101	US HIGHWAY
138	OREGON HIGHWAY
······	REGION BOUNDARY

IDAHO

3	Spring Getaways 1–12
17A	Summer Getaways 13–24
26A	Fall Getaways 25–36
45	Winter Getaways 37-48

NEVADA

Acknowledgments

When I sit behind the wheel of my truck to begin a day's travel to some new destination, I am always hopeful that at some point in the latest adventure I get to travel down a road or lane that somehow managed to fall off the map. Perhaps through chance, but more often with a county road map and curiosity, I have found some of my most interesting stories just wandering where the pavement leads. Charles Kuralt described it best: "I fell in love with little roads, the ones without names or numbers." Put me in his camp, for it's often where you'll find me searching for adventures. Frankly, I am giddy as a kid to think that my "office" is some rural roadway that requires a bit more time to experience; especially the sort of pike that my dad, Grant Sr., relished when I was a kid—a roadway that's windy and springy and narrow. He would steer the family wagon close to the edge of a slim mountain road and yell, "Whoaooooo!"

"Ah, Dad, stop that!" would come the cry from each of the three little kids in the backseat—while Mom gave a furtive glance to Dad and then to the side of the road that seemed to fall away in a deep canyon.

"Do it again, Dad! Do it again," we cried. We just couldn't get enough of his teasing—not reckless—just a feeling of freedom that comes from the open road on a day too nice to stay indoors. You must slow down to drive these types of roads and that's when the fun begins. Perhaps that's why I have such a love affair with backdoor byways; they always take a bit longer to get from this place to that and during the journey my youthful memories are reborn.

Reporters are charged with the task of shaping and funneling the facts, relying on gut instincts and insights about a place, a person, or an issue to tell their stories. Perhaps they will add in a bit of feeling to complement the pictures that really tell the story. You see, without the pictures, the television reporter might as well go fishing! Fortunately, my *Grant's Getaways* television production partner, photographer Jeff Kastner, enjoys doing both. He does a superb job capturing the finest getaway moments and his keen eye and artistic touch with a camera and film are humbling . . . all of which makes my writing much, much easier. I hope you enjoy the colorful images in this book. They are all Jeff Kastner's.

My sincere thanks to the Travel Oregon management team for their trust and confidence in me to represent Oregon—including CEO Todd Davidson, Mo Sherifdeen, Kevin Wright, and Emily Forsha. I also thank David Lane of the Oregon Department of Fish and Wildlife, Ashley Massey of the Oregon State Marine Board, and Chris Havel of the Oregon Parks and Recreation Department. I appreciate their insights, advice, and story suggestions. Further, I extend my deep gratitude to the KGW-TV management team including DJ Wilson, Brenda Buratti, and News Director Rick Jacobs. Each continues to embrace and encourage our work at every turn. In fact, all of these folks support the *Grant's Getaways* endeavors and allow me the privilege of travel across the region. I also thank the folks at Graphic Arts Books for the chance to continue telling my stories from the great Oregon outdoors, including Doug Pfeiffer, Kathy Howard, Vicki Knapton, and Angie Zbornik. I especially thank Michelle Blair for her outstanding copy-editing skills and for improving my manuscript at every turn.

Introduction

*N*ow, Grant, I want you to stay right on my tail, there's no room for mistakes in this cave, and as you can see by the opening, the space starts out fairly wide and tall but shrinks to elbow 'n belly-time real fast! Oh, and uhhh, you're not claustrophobic are you?" Dave Immel, Oregon Department of Fish and Wildlife biologist, half smiled as we stared into the pitch-black of a moss-shrouded cave in the Willamette National Forest. News photographer Mike Rosborough and I had joined Immel's research team in the dead of winter in Oregon's Cascade Mountain wilderness. The team's mission was to track down several black bears during winter hibernation to change out the batteries that powered the radio collars on each of the bears. The collars had been attached during previous summer trapping events and were a critical tool in monitoring black bear behaviors over the long term. Specifically, the scientists were trying to better understand the kinds of habitats that black bears preferred throughout the year. Rosborough and I figured this would be a fine story; it was not only timely, but offered a different slant on the Oregon snow country and provided unique video about seldom seen wildlife behavior. Viewers could also gain a better understanding of the lengths that wildlife biologists must go to learn more about species.

For the record, here's a significant lesson that three-plus decades of covering wildlife stories has taught me: expect the unexpected! Critters in the wild are the most daunting story subjects to capture with a camera and I've plenty of photography partners in the TV news business who will testify to that frustration. We have spent countless hours—no, make that days—traveling across hundreds of miles, often in the worst winter weather, hoping to capture just the right moment when a wild animal might display some unique behavior: be it salmon jumping a waterfall, sage grouse strutting across their springtime desert leks (breeding grounds), whales breeching in the ocean, or a hike into distant, craggy mountains for the rare chance to see cougar juveniles. I have learned that when it comes to encountering wildlife, it often pays to be a lucky rather than an accomplished journalist.

Despite knowing that critters never keep appointments, I must have ignored that adage on this bear story because the story sounded like such a piece of cake! After all, Immel knew exactly where this bear was sleeping, deep beyond the maw of the cave's entrance, and his plan seemed simple enough: he and I would crawl inside the cave and find the bear. Immel would carry a tranquilizing injection dart on the end of a 6-foot-long wand, while I would handle a Minicam attached to a short rod that would allow us to see the action as Immel exchanged the radio collar's batteries. He would also inspect the bear's overall health and in all likelihood, we'd capture a unique piece of video for an intriguing story that viewers would find educational and entertaining. "This particular bear will be a good one for you to document," said Immel. "We've monitored his movements the past three seasons and he's particularly fond of this cave during winter—and he is almost always in deep hibernation."

And so, the adventure began, Immel in the lead, slowly and quietly, hunkered over and nearly crouching as each of us shuffled forward, into the dark. The biologist soon turned on his headlamp and dropped to his knees. I followed suit and found myself staring at the soles of Immel's boots as we crawled along the cave floor. I noted that the cave's ceiling was dropping quickly. Immel whispered, "I can't quite see the bear yet, but I can sure smell him." I could too! The musky smell of a wild animal is hard to mistake and I also noted how dry, even warm, the cave habitat seemed; a perfect place to sleep away a bone-chilling winter.

By my calculations, I have written and produced thousands of segments and programs on the great Oregon outdoors since the early 1980s, stories that required countless hours traveling the state's back roads and byways and here's a little secret: I have loved every minute of it. Despite the physical challenges of climbing, crawling, swimming, or hiking to find fish and wildlife in their natural habitats, there's a certain joy that results from a successful search and the knowledge that we might teach our viewers something they didn't know about their region. As a result, I've learned to admire our varied and wonderful wildlife: deer, elk, bald eagles, and fish species too: the salmon, trout, and the long-lived sturgeon. I suppose the beauty of travel is the unexpected treasures that I have found along the way, treasures measured in the memories of sights and sounds that have connected this small town kid to his home state in ways that I only dreamed about as a boy.

We were now down to those "elbows and bellies" that Immel had warned me about earlier. We were crawling inside the ever-shrinking cave and it was definitely not a place for anyone who had a fear of tight quarters. My biggest challenge was keeping the camera up above my head and pointed toward Immel. I was hoping to get usable video clips of the action as we slid along on our bellies. I could just make out in the bouncing headlight the frame of a large furry mass a mere 20 feet or so ahead of us when Immel suddenly stopped—went silent for a moment and then uttered two words a television producer never, ever wants to hear: "Uh, oh!"

"Uh, oh what?" I urgently whispered back. "What is it? What's wrong? Is it the bear? Can I get a shot?" Immel was motionless and silent, as was I. In the quiet of the cave I thought I could hear a low, guttural sound, not quite a growl but more like a long sleepy yawn. Immel urgently whispered, "Move back!" And then in a commanding tone: "The bear is awake! Move back NOW!"

It isn't often that my news-gathering work intersects with moments of fear, danger, or sheer terror, but every now and then the aha moments hit: spontaneous seconds when the responsibility to deliver stories to viewers seems in a precarious balance with my own health and safety. I have known aha moments before: jumping out of a perfectly good airplane on a skydiving story, climbing Smith Rock's signature Monkey Face when the ground suddenly seemed a million miles away, or a stare down with a large cougar along Catherine Creek in Union County. There have been significant weather-related events too: full-blown floods, hurricane-force windstorms, or too-close-for-comfort lightning strikes, when the better part of my valor, my safety, seemed like a quick retreat.

This was one of those moments. But, as challenging as it was to get into the cave, it was next to impossible to turn around and exit, so it was "bellies 'n elbows" again—only backwards! Huffing and puffing and inching backwards as quickly as possible, I was soon able to rise to my knees. I checked the camera rod so as not to stick the biologist in the rear and then I was up to my feet and finally out through the cave's opening. All the while, I could hear the bear's rumbling and growling as it closed in. Immel was right behind me and in a flash his team immediately draped a canvas tarp across the cave opening and pulled it tight. The plan was to keep the bear inside the cave, so I grabbed a corner of the tarp and the six of us held fast! In a heartbeat, the bear was there—just on the other side of the canvas. I could see his jaws working across the other side of the tarp—chomping down, trying to get a tooth-hold on the fabric and rip it to shreds. It grunted and growled and chopped and Immel was faced with a dilemma: how to deliver the tranquilizer to an obviously wide-awake, riled-up black bear who was not going to lie down and fall fast asleep anytime soon.

"OK, let's let it go, no choice," said Immel. "Drop the far corner, move out of the way, and we'll let it go on 1-2-3!" It was not an easy decision for Immel, especially considering the time and energy that the team expended to hike to the remote site. Still, the biologist didn't have much choice. So, in a moment (really the only moment for photographer Mike Rosborough) and as soon as a team member dropped the far corner of the tarp, we watched a black bear's back end fly down the steep hillside in a blur of forest duff. The bear was gone and—my heart was racing from one of the closest encounters I have ever had with a wild animal.

It has always been my hope that *Grant's Getaways* viewers learn something about Oregon that they didn't know before. For gosh sakes, why live here if you don't go searching for those singular moments that set Oregon apart from just about everywhere else? My hope for this *Guide to Wildlife Watching in Oregon* is that you will explore Oregon's special places to see the state's truest native residents. The book spans the varied geophysical regions of the state and includes fish- and wildlife-based adventures for each month of the year. In this text, I offer many of my finest and favorite experiences covering Oregon fish and wildlife stories and issues during my career as a broadcast journalist. To be clear, some of my stories and destinations are revisited from previous essays, while there are many more new stories and locations to guide you to forty-eight destinations during what I consider their seasonal peaks. There are also many new sidebars that offer choice locations, tips and tactics, recipes, and anecdotal stories to give you a behind-the-scenes glimpse into my work. These are places I have especially enjoyed at a particular time of year. But let me be clear: These are but my favorite times to visit, so don't get the notion they don't shine at other times of the year.

I have often considered my news-gathering work akin to a class that could be called "Wildlife 101" and my point is to now share with you some really fabulous opportunities to see and experience Oregon's fish and wildlife. So please think of this book as a classroom, for we learn the meaning of a "convocation" of eagles, and see the results of one man's quest to create a spectacular collection of azaleas and rhododendrons at Oregon's Secret Garden. We paddle along a watery wildlife trail to catch a glimpse of the Oregon state animal at Beaver Creek State Natural Area, and admire the dedication of a woman who helps Oregon's sick and injured wildlife at her hospital for the wild. We climb aboard a helicopter and fly across the Cascade Mountains to deliver flying fish to Oregon's high lakes. Speaking of heights, we climb an iron giant and see the most astounding collection of summer wildflowers I've ever enjoyed. We follow Lewis and Clark's trail along the lower Columbia River and explore a rare, unchanged swamp and forest. We also marvel at the remarkably entertaining behavior of Sauvie Island's colorful sandhill cranes. You can join me for a hike to a remote stretch of the Salmonberry River to see how wild steelhead must jump a 10-foot waterfall in order to reach their spawning grounds. We visit Astoria to learn more about the century-old craftsmanship that keeps the Dungeness crabbing fishery afloat, and then we follow a steady stream of small fish called smelt that charge up the Columbia River by the millions each winter. Speaking of fish, I cannot overstate the popularity of our *Getaways* cooking segments, so I have included more recipes from my kitchen that center on lip-smacking crab, bay clams, salmon, and more—these recipes will impress your friends with true Oregon flair.

These *Getaways* selections offer my favorite wildlife experiences that have kept my photographers on their toes through the decades. Many of the walks are accessible on a tank of gas, while others require more planning and time. I also describe interesting side trips, as well as more science and travel strategies than I am able to share during my weekly television programs. I mention wheelchair accessibility where available, although there is almost always a path or trail nearby that can be navigated in a wheelchair. The point of all this, as I like to tell folks in person, on the air, or in writing, is just to get out there, enjoy Oregon any time of year, and make some memories of your own. I hope my *Guide to Wildlife Watching in Oregon* will help show the way.

Spring

Grant McOmie's Outdoor Talk—
The Nature of People and Wildlife

I have been the luckiest reporter in the world and never more so than in the late 1990s when I realized that two career paths could smoothly merge into something new for our viewers. You see, it had always bugged me that I wasn't doing more to take advantage of the wealth of priceless wildlife video we had accumulated in the station's video library. It seemed some of our best critter moments aired but one time and then the tapes were relegated to the dusty basement, where chances were good the video would not be seen or heard from again. I am certain that I complained loudly about this on the home front too because after a few

weeks of listening to my ranting about how the station should do this or should do that to better utilize resources and promote the outdoors, my wife, Christine, reminded me that I had started my professional career as a teacher when she said: "So why don't you do what you do well; craft a lesson plan about wildlife and then suggest to management that they consider something new."

Her suggestion was simple, direct, and it was brilliant. And so, a few weeks later, "Outdoor Talk" was launched. Through the new program, I scheduled a different classroom each week, students ranging from fifth grade through high school, and presented a one-hour wildlife lesson. The lesson centered on our region's endangered species and how each of us could do more to protect them. The centerpiece of my visits was a short video that showed off the varied fish and wildlife species that live in Oregon and were at risk of extinction. The sessions also solicited students' concerns, ideas, and questions about the wildlife that lived in our own backyards. It was a remarkable 4-year experience that allowed me to visit with thousands of youngsters, and it also led to one of the most fascinating wildlife stories of my career.

The phone rang on a cold, damp March afternoon and the caller identified herself as "Eleanor." She explained that her great-granddaughter had raved about my recent Outdoor Talk with her sixth-grade class and she hoped that I might be the "answer to her prayers." It seemed Eleanor had a bit of a wildlife problem, and she didn't know how to solve it. Nor did she want to explain too many details over the phone, other than she had lived in the same southeast Portland neighborhood for many decades and could I possibly "come over to my home today and see what I'm up against."

Urban wildlife problems were nothing new to me. In fact, I'd covered scores of so-called nuisance wildlife issues—from skunks and squirrels and small birds that moved in with their human neighbors, to garbage-can bears and pet-eating cougars that were right at home in the suburbs, to elk and deer that loved to eat rose bushes and trample garden plants. Most of the time, these conflicts resulted from human sprawl creeping into areas that had been wildlife habitats. The animals were usually drugged or trapped and then transported somewhere else or even euthanized to permanently solve what was actually a human-caused problem. There was rarely a good ending for the critters.

My photographer, Cliff Ellis, joined me for the short ride to Eleanor's home and in quick order we were standing on the broad wooden porch of a 1930s bungalow-style cottage. The front door opened and we were warmly greeted by an elderly woman with a pleasant smile. But I quickly sensed something more, a shadow of worry, perhaps even fear in both her expression and tone: "Grant, I am so happy you could come over so soon," and then she shot a quick glance to a nearby wall clock. "We haven't much time—let me show you the problem!" Eleanor welcomed us into her home and led us to the back of her house, through a doorway that linked the kitchen with a screened-off porch. I gazed around the comfy confines of the room and noticed a half dozen 40-pound bags of dog food, stacked like cordwood in a far corner. "Where are your dogs, Eleanor?" I was curious because I saw no signs of a pet in the home, just the generous ration of dog food. As Cliff set up his tripod and camera, Eleanor explained that the food was for a different kind of animal and we were about to have a front row seat to "something that just got out of hand."

"Come over here, Grant, and look at my yard—they'll be here anytime," said the elderly woman. I moved to the door, nudged it open, held the spring-loaded screen, and gazed across her generous yard. I noticed three or four large trees—cherry trees. Each soared 40 feet into the sky; they'd stood in her yard a long time. There was a curtain of smaller shrubbery along the property's perimeter and the entire landscape was orderly and well designed. A sprawling lawn stretched way back, perhaps 200 feet, to a white wooden fence. In fact, the entire large lot was enclosed by a sturdy 6-foot-tall cedar fence. "My husband took great care of the yard. It was his passion. So were the wildlife that were drawn here—especially the birds," said Eleanor. "I guess some of that carried over to me after he passed 5 years ago, 'cuz that's when it started."

I nodded and asked, "When what started?"

"At first there were only five or six," she replied. "They looked so hungry and so miserable during that cold, wet winter. It was a winter that just wouldn't end. Oh, what time is it, Grant?"

I looked down at my watch and answered, "About five."

"OK. Get ready," she said cautiously. I glanced at Ellis who looked at me with a disbelief that seemed to say, Tell me again, why are we here?

I stared down the long greenway to the back fence and thought I could discern movement of a sort—a dark, wavy line seemed to grow across the top of the sturdy fence. And that wasn't all. Along the back corners and from the tall cherry trees there was more movement, but in the fading light it was tough to get a clear view of the things, and there were many—things, that moved. And then suddenly, the things hit the ground and were loping toward us.

"OK, watch out, Grant," said Eleanor, who scurried past me to the corner, reached inside the one open bag of dog food, pulled out a large bowl full of the dry cubes, and rushed back to the screen door.

It was a tsunami of black, brown, and gray furry critters—raccoons—and they raced toward the back porch. She opened the door, tossed out the food, and snapped the door shut again. The tidal wave of fur crashed across the yard, just feet from the door. There were raccoons everywhere, chowing down on the dog food. "I have to give them whatever they want or they'll start knocking on the door," said Eleanor.

I'd never seen so many squirming, writhing raccoons and I tried to count them, "Twenty-four . . . twenty-six . . . thirty-two . . . thirty-eight . . . forty-two . . . my gosh, Eleanor! How many raccoons do you feed?"

I stopped counting at forty-eight and then just stared at the unbelievable wildlife scene. Ellis looked up from his camera eyepiece and nodded with a smile. He was in heaven as one of the larger raccoons waddled toward the door, stood on its hind legs, and seemed to wave at us with its front paws. "Look at those teeth," said Ellis. "He's grinning at us . . . or smiling . . . or something."

Eleanor quickly opened the door and tossed out another bowl of dog food.

"That's one of the biggest, boldest raccoons I've ever seen," I quipped. The raccoon seemed huge as a house and it was also lightning quick as it snapped at the flying food and then turned its backside to us and gorged itself.

"You see my problem?" she asked. "The number of raccoons keeps growing and I can't afford to do this every day. I probably go through three bags each week. It's expensive and my family insists that I stop spending my money on raccoon food."

"Well, Eleanor, I do have a solution but frankly, given what I see here this afternoon, you are not going to like it," I said. I slowly and deliberately explained to her that in order for wildlife to stay wild people cannot, must not, ever feed them. Period. "Raccoons in particular easily habituate to the kindness of humans and will continue to return day after day to take advantage of the routine you've provided," I explained.

"Oh, won't they starve if I stop?" she asked.

"Absolutely not. Raccoons are intelligent and forage for all kinds of food in the wild. They are omnivores. They eat anything, and there is no shortage of food for them. And if you don't stop, your problem will get even bigger. Do you want that?"

"Ohhhhh, noooo!" was her reply. "Enough is enough, and I'll try."

I thought long and hard about the amazing video that Ellis shot that afternoon and my interview with a homeowner who had her hands full of a nuisance wildlife scenario that she created. The critters were in control of Eleanor. She was living an expensive nightmare that turned the human-wildlife relationship upside down. Eventually, I opted not to air the story of a grandmother who was carried away by kindness and created a neighborhood nuisance. I didn't want to embarrass her or her family. I gave her the name and number of the local state wildlife biologist and told her I'd check in with her from time to time. I did speak with Eleanor again a few weeks later when she called me with an update: she had "cut back" on the amount of dog food that she tossed out her backdoor. As a result, the raccoon numbers had declined in her yard. She told me her goal was to eventually stop feeding them all together, but that it was too hard to go cold turkey. She also told me she appreciated that we didn't air her story. I wished her all the best. More than 20 year later, I still find the Eleanor experience not only humorous, but instructive and revealing about our view of wildlife and the natural world. We care about them, we want them around us, but we sometimes overstep and interfere, and that usually leads to unforeseen consequences.

1

Dancing Antlers and Oregon's Secret Garden

*T*he beauty of an Oregon spring is the chance to strike out on new adventures where the scenery is never twice the same. So it is at two striking sites for the price of one stop along Oregon State Highway 38 near Reedsport. The first is hard to miss while the second depends upon good timing and patience—let's begin with what appear to be the dancing antlers across grassy fields at the Dean Creek Elk Viewing Area.

On some days, elk antlers are all you spy from the refuge viewpoint in the tall, wavy grass that obscures the large animals that lounge across the habitat at Dean Creek. The site encompasses 1,040 acres and it is jointly managed by the Bureau of Land Management (BLM) and the Oregon Department of Fish and Wildlife (ODFW). It is managed for public viewing and education with information kiosks at the O. H. Hinsdale Interpretive Center. The covered view site offers information about Oregon's Roosevelt elk and the environment of the Dean Creek area as well as spotting scopes to enhance viewing. There are also free brochures that tell you the story of the elk and the surrounding area.

BLM Manager Bob Golden said that it's a reliable photo opportunity because the elk are so close at hand—often, the big animals (some elk tip the scales at 600 pounds) are but a few yards away, so you'll want to have your camera at your side: "We offer visitors a great educational experience and you do get to see the wildlife up close. On any given day you can come out here and see the elk."

The elk have lived in the Dean Creek Wildlife Area since the 1930s when historic salt marshes were drained and freshwater was allowed to feed the site's grasslands. The herd of 120 Roosevelt elk roams freely on protected pastures, woodlands, and wetland areas, sharing their habitat with other wildlife including bald eagles, Canada geese, beaver, and black-tailed deer.

Don't forget your camera to capture the colorful collection of rhodies at Oregon's Secret Garden.

But Dean Creek's elk herd is just the start of this wild adventure. The real showstopper is just up the road at Spruce Reach Island where you see thousands of rhododendrons and azaleas and camellias—over 300 different species. Stroll in and discover what some call "Oregon's Secret Garden." "It was a bit of a secret garden for decades," said Bob MacIntyre—member of the American Rhododendron Society and a Friend of the Hinsdale Garden. "You see all of that and more here: white, cream, pink, reds, oranges, yellows, and purples. There are rhodies of every imaginable color, size, and texture." It's a public place built by a private man.

Howard Hinsdale was a successful Oregon businessman who began transforming his 55-acre Spruce Reach Island right after World War II. "It is unlike any garden you've ever visited," noted Megan Harper—a BLM staff member. "Most people are familiar with more manicured English garden styles, but you come here and it's like a wild garden. Hinsdale spent a lot of time planning and putting this garden together in a very specific way."

Hinsdale imported rare rhodies and giant spruce trees from as far away as England too. He barged them through the Panama Canal and had them delivered to his island. Harper said that he even "strolled and shopped" through many Portland-area neighborhoods. "If he found a rhodie that he loved, he'd knock on the door and start peeling off bills and say, 'How much would it take to give me that plant?' And then his crew would take shovels and dig it up right on the spot." Hinsdale created an oasis of calm on his island but it took 20 years of hard work to achieve. "You must understand," added MacIntyre, "this was swampland. He had to dredge the Umpqua River through this stretch and deposit the material—28,000 cubic yards of silt—onto his island. Plus, the scores of old spruce trees that you see rising above it all—he bought them all and planted each one here."

But when he was done, here was Hinsdale's escape from the hectic hubbub and stressful business life. "Oh, he was a driven man to be sure," said MacIntyre. "Just imagine trying to do this work. He was probably driven in his business, but he could come here and leave all of that way out there." Hinsdale's secret garden lasted until 1994. "And then the government bought it," said Stephan Samuels, a BLM archaeologist. "When we found out what we had, we went to work on it and began to open it up because that's what Mr. Hinsdale did." Samuels added that through the decades, Hinsdale had shared his garden with friends and family who loved the place in spring—that tradition continues today. "It is here for people to enjoy," added Harper. "You don't honor the place by keeping it a secret or not letting people enjoy it."

The BLM has recently teamed up with a local Friends of Hinsdale Garden. They plan to open the place throughout the spring and summer so more visitors can see and appreciate one Oregonian's vision for peace and solitude. "We hope to open it from April through October," added Samuels, "even when it's not blooming, people can come here, relax, and have a nice lunch while they enjoy a beautiful spot on the Umpqua River." "It was a secret garden, but now it's a spectacular place for anyone to enjoy," said MacIntyre with a smile. "You walk in here and, oh my gosh, it's awesome! That's what Hinsdale was after and I think he achieved it."

---

1 Dean Creek Elk Viewing Area

Where: 48819 State Highway 38, Reedsport, OR 97467

Web: www.dfw.state.or.us

Phone: BLM: 541-756-0100; US Fish and Wildlife Service: 541-888-5515

Watch the Episode: www.traveloregon.com/oregonsecretgarden

2

Lend a Hand at Oregon's All-Volunteer Hatchery

*A*s the sun makes itself more at home across Oregon, April is a time of year to head outdoors for on-the-water adventures, and if there's a more exciting fishing moment than hooking and fighting a chrome bright chinook salmon fresh from the sea, I surely don't know what it could be. That's especially true on Tillamook Bay where an early morning flood tide brings a torrent of spring chinook—fresh from the ocean—in a rush up the estuary where anglers wait—with baited lines.

The fish are special, what many call Oregon's premier salmon, and are prized for their high oil content and rich, buttery taste. In Tillamook County, a dedicated group of Oregonians roll up their sleeves to join a labor of love at Netarts Bay; over 400 volunteers show huge heart and commitment to help Oregon's all-volunteer fish hatchery called Whiskey Creek. Located in southern Tillamook County and hugging the shoreline at Netarts Bay, the Whiskey Creek Salmon Hatchery raises more than a quarter million spring and fall chinook salmon each year and it is open to visitors every day.

Admission is free at Whiskey Creek Hatchery and it's open every day so you can explore the grounds along Netarts Bay.

"We're all volunteer and always have been and always will be," noted Jerry Dove, a longtime hatchery supporter who has been at the helm of the operation since it began in 1987. The Tillamook Anglers Association has

More than 400 volunteers lend a hand on fin clipping day at Whiskey Creek Hatchery.

owned and managed the hatchery since the late 1980s. Memberships and donations keep the operation afloat while the Oregon Department of Fish and Wildlife (ODFW) supplies the fish.

"It's a great partnership," said ODFW Biologist Rick Klumph. "We provide the technical oversight and they do all the physical manpower of raising the fish. It's a productive partnership with our agency." Each spring, Dove guides hundreds of people who put on rubber gloves and carefully grab a fistful of slippery, wiggly baby salmon. They must carefully clip the adipose fin from each of 105,000 spring salmon. The fin clip distinguishes the fish so anglers can tell the difference between hatchery and wild salmon.

"The fish are asleep. Each one of them rests in an anesthetic bath before we clip the adipose. The scissor clip is quick and easy," added Dove. The adipose fin is a small, half moon–shaped fin that's just behind the dorsal fin and just in front of the tail fin. It's a fin that the fish doesn't need to survive. "There's a lot of mentoring and we try to hook up a newcomer with a veteran," added Klumph. "It's not difficult, but there's definitely a technique to it."

Volunteer Alvin Saul has been helping the Whiskey Creek Hatchery from the start and he said he likes the chance to catch up with longtime friends who feel like they're making a difference for other anglers. "They need the support, and if I stayed home and nobody showed up, we'd end up with thousands of fish that wouldn't get clipped. So, we make a difference."

Whiskey Creek Hatchery is 2 miles from one of Oregon's finest parklands:

Cape Lookout State Park, where there is always something new to do. You may enjoy a beachside stroll or an overnight campout in a yurt, or take a hike to the end of Cape Lookout where—this time of year—the gray whale migration south from the Bering Sea is at its peak. "We are a tourist attraction," said Dove. "We're so close to so many activities and we draw more than 125,000 visitors each year."

"It gives folks a good feeling to lend a hand to the hatchery operation," added Klumph. "Plus, in a couple of years they can go out and try to catch an adult salmon from Tillamook Bay, so it's a great program all the way around." Whiskey Creek Hatchery is on Netarts Bay. Drive to Tillamook and follow the signs to Cape Lookout State Park. The hatchery is 2 miles north of the park.

2A Whiskey Creek Hatchery

Where: 7660 Whiskey Creek Road, Tillamook, OR 97141

Web: www.ifish.net/Tillanglers

Phone: 503-815-2566

2B Cape Lookout State Park

Where: 13000 Whiskey Creek Road W, Tillamook, OR 97141

Web: www.oregonstateparks.org

Phone: 503-842-4981 or 800-551-6949

Watch the Episode: www.traveloregon.com/whiskeycreek

3

Home on the Antelope Range

*T*he landscape surrounding the Hart Mountain National Antelope Refuge in south-central Oregon is remote by any stretch of the imagination, and it is a place filled with contrasts: it is not a classic, snowcapped peak but more a massive, volcanic ridge jutting above the desert. Its west side soars sharply from the Warner Valley floor to nearly a mile high via a series of rugged cliffs and steep ridges. The east side is rounded, gentler, and easier to traverse. And it is distant—hundreds of miles from the nearest town of any size—yet, for all its loneliness, if you wait patiently and watch carefully, you may be taken aback by the number of foraging herds of pronghorn antelope, families of bighorn sheep, and mule deer, plus flocks of sage grouse that make the refuge home.

At its western base, another gathering occurs each year when several dozen wildlife experts from state and federal agencies come together in a fascinating project called the California Bighorn Sheep Roundup. It's a capture-and-transplant project that's now moving into its fourth decade, and it's made the difference in restoring a species that was once near the brink of extinction. Original herds of the California bighorn sheep, a species native to the western United States, disappeared from Oregon in the 1920s as a result of competition with livestock for food, too much hunting, and too many people building farms, ranches, and

Helicopters have proven efficient and effective tools for bighorn sheep round-ups since the 1980s.

homesteads across the desert. But the bighorns scored some success in 1954 when a herd of twenty sheep was successfully reintroduced to the federally managed refuge. The herds were protected on the refuge and they have thrived. The year I visited the project for a special news report, I quickly discovered that the heart of the bighorn sheep roundup is teamwork and technology. The former comes through cooperative participation and the expertise of state and federal wildlife biologists, plus staff and volunteers from several sport and conservation organizations. The technology is in the form of a Bell 206 Jet Ranger helicopter that makes capture of the elusive animals easier. During my visit, the plan was to capture up to fifty bighorns that were to be moved to four other Oregon sites.

State wildlife biologist Jim Torland told me that the helicopter makes the otherwise impossible job possible. "When you're going after the bighorns, you must go where they live," he explained. "This is such unforgiving, difficult country to cover on foot, and it's impossible with vehicles, so the chopper allows us access up narrow defiles, canyons, and steep slopes. If we can find the sheep on the flats at the top of the mountain, man, then it's all gravy at that point."

As news photographer Bob Jaundalderis and I climbed aboard the ship to document the capture, I could see every aspect of this annual Hart Mountain Bighorn Sheep Roundup (BSR) depended upon teamwork, especially between the helicopter pilot and his "gunner," the person who sits strapped into the ship near the open side door. The gunner and the pilot are in constant radio contact, as each scans the landscape for the bighorn herds. Once spotted, the twosome chooses an animal—either a male or female—and descends to just yards above it, then speeds with it across the ground. The gunner selects just the right animal and then fires his handheld "net gun." This high-tech tool, cradled and shoulder mounted just as a hunter might handle a rifle, utilizes a .30-caliber blank cartridge.

When fired, the blank propels four weighted ends of a heavyweight 15-square-foot mesh net. The weights are brass cylinders that shoot out and open the net in the air. It then descends around the animal like a huge bag. It is a fascinating capture process and it happens in a heartbeat, but the effort takes precise timing and no small amount of courage for both the pilot and the gunner. After all, the sheep are fast—and elusive—as they dart across the ground at speeds reaching 30 miles an hour.

Once an animal has been enveloped by the giant net, a critical third team member, called a "mugger," immediately jumps from the ship to the ground. He hobbles the animal's front and hind legs with leather straps and bindings to protect himself and the animal from harm. Then a critical period begins as the mugger monitors the sheep's temperature. The sheep's temperature is a reliable indication of its stress level. If it's above 107 degrees, the mugger must cool the animal with ice-cold water. I watched as a ewe, a young female, was cooled with canteen

Wildlife technicians work quietly and quickly as they prep the bighorn sheep for transport to their new homes.

water and then carefully loaded into another, larger ventilated mesh bag for transport. Within minutes, the whoosh-whoosh-whoosh of the chopper's blades was heard, signaling its return. A cable was dropped from the ship, which the mugger attached to the bagged animal. Slowly and carefully, the animal was lifted into the cream-colored sky and then flown back to base camp.

Challenged by steep terrain, howling winds, and temperatures that can drop to 30 degrees below 0, the BSR is certainly a test of teamwork, but it's teamwork that doesn't end with the capture, for it continues as the animal is gently dropped into the waiting arms of the biologists at base camp. Speaking little and only in hushed tones, each team of four scientists works quickly and efficiently on each captured sheep. Like a precise, well-schooled machine, the crews continue to monitor the bighorn's body temperature, collect blood samples, and then inject each animal with antibiotics to protect it against infections. An ear tag is also attached to each sheep to help with later identification. Retired state wildlife biologist George Keister explained to me that every effort is made to ease the animal's stress: "We want the animals as calm as we can keep them through the entire process. Many, many studies over the years have shown that, given our level of care following capture, this procedure has the lowest immediate and long-term stress compared to other capture methods on these animals." It's also the most efficient method.

While the helicopter capture project is expensive, the costs are offset by the sale of hunting licenses, tags, and permits. Once hunted to near extinction, the California bighorn numbers now exceed 5,000 in more than forty sites across Eastern Oregon. It's a special program, blending human technology with a commitment to restore a species.

I hope your visit to Hart Mountain National Antelope Refuge is as exciting as mine have been over the years. I have learned that each season offers something new and special to see and experience. Binoculars or a spotting scope is a must for seeing bighorn sheep and other wildlife from either the base of Hart Mountain on the way into the refuge from the west or from Flook Knoll, 8 miles east of refuge headquarters. All camping is located at the Hot Springs campground, 4 miles south of refuge headquarters. Located within the campground is the Hot Springs bathhouse, which consists of a hot spring enclosed in a cement building for year-round use. There are two pit toilets and both are wheelchair accessible. No RV hookups, no drinking water, and no firewood are to be found. Free permits are required for all overnight stays. The permits are self-issued at refuge headquarters (open 24 hours a day), where there is also a restroom. No gas is available at Hart Mountain.

A bit of good news: there is abundant wildlife. The best way to see sheep, antelope, or deer is to take a daylong hike into one of the canyons from the base of the mountain. Keep in mind that there are no hiking trails, but some graded roads can be walked or driven. Warning: The roads are rough and rugged, so you must be prepared to be on your own in a wilderness setting for an extended time. Four-wheel-drive vehicles are highly recommended.

---

3 Hart Mountain National Antelope Refuge

Where: 38782 Hart Mountain Road, Plush, OR 97637

Web: www.fws.gov/Sheldonhartmtn

Phone: 541-947-2731

4

Suburban Nature Parks

*I*n early spring, more people explore the great outdoors and it's rather remarkable that the best places to start are often just down the road beyond the next hill. My favorite walks on the wild side are often just off the back porch and closer than you think. For example, at Hillsboro's Jackson Bottom Wetlands Preserve you'll find wildlife at every turn: a solitary eagle perched on watch, scurrying shorebirds probing the muck of the marshes, or V-shaped flocks winging from this place to that. Less than 20 miles from Portland, Jackson Bottom Wetlands is about as grassroots as it gets, according to education specialist Sarah Pinnock: "People come here and want to learn about wildlife and wetlands so we make that opportunity available to them in any way we can because we really like that."

Born in the 1980s of a partnership between the city of Hillsboro, local citizens, and the Oregon Department of Fish and Wildlife, it transformed 700 acres of wasteland into a wildlife paradise. The preserve's wetlands and trails surround an education center where hands-on exhibits teach you about the environment. In the middle you will see that a massive eagle nest rules this roost. "The nest was cut out of a dead cottonwood tree several years ago," noted the preserve's manager, Ed Becker. "It was abandoned by the bald eagles and now provides

The eagle nest was recovered intact before the tree fell down and measures over 10 feet tall and 6 feet wide.

Sunrise is the best time to explore Jackson Bottom Wetlands for that's when the wildlife are most active.

a unique exhibit; sort of a centerpiece for us and just a wonderful thing to have."

Twenty miles away as the eagle flies, discover what I like to call a "back pocket wilderness": Tualatin Hills Nature Park, a 222-acre oasis of wildness in the heart of Beaverton that is prized for many reasons. The parkland offers miles of paved and soft surface trails and two creeks (Beaverton Creek and Cedar Mill Creek) that merge inside the park to provide water everywhere. No need to worry about getting your feet wet, though, for a wheelchair accessible boardwalk rises above the wetlands to give you easy passage.

You can duck in and escape foul weather at the park's education center for hands-on exhibits and classrooms. "It's beautiful with views out to the forest and on occasion we even get deer walking past," noted education manager Kristin Atman. "When the kids are out from school we offer programs and we have tons of spring break camps planned for kids aged 4 through 11." Park ranger Greg Creager added that the birds and frogs offer plenty of the natural "sounds of spring" and signal that warmer times are just around the bend at a place you should visit as soon as you can: "It's really such a special place—a wild place in the middle of an urban and suburban area; something we're pretty lucky to have in Beaverton."

Consider yourself lucky when you discover the new trails and jaw-dropping views atop the nearby Cooper Mountain Nature Park. "I think that's the most common reaction when you visit Cooper Mountain for the first time," said park ranger

Scott Hinderman: "'Wow, what a view!' It's one of those undiscovered gems. We are surrounded by a vast sea of urban area in this part of Washington County and all of a sudden you have this little island up here."

More than 3 miles of trails for exploring a unique pine and Doug fir upland forest that also contains unique and prized white oak savanna areas. "Deer are common up here and raptors are a favorite," added Hinderman. "Red-tailed hawks are easy to spot this time of year and the owls are more often heard hooting too. Best time to hear them is early in the morning or just before dusk."

The new Cooper Mountain Education Center offers classroom space and a full suite of activities are available on the weekends for youngsters and adults. But for the most part, folks come to the Cooper Mountain Nature Park to get away from it all. Hinderman added that the best part is you won't have far to travel to reach the site either: "There are many people who come up here just to sit on a bench and enjoy the solitude. This is one of the quieter places in the Beaverton area and visitors like it that way."

4A Jackson Bottom Wetlands

Where: 2600 SW Hillsboro Highway, Hillsboro, OR 97123

Web: www.jacksonbottom.org

Phone: 503-681-6206

4B Tualatin Hills Nature Park

Where: 15655 SW Millikan Way, Beaverton, OR 97003

Web: www.thprd.org

Phone: 503-629-6350

4C Cooper Mountain Nature Park

Where: 18892 SW Kemmer Road, Beaverton, OR 97007

Web: www.oregonmetro.gov/parks/cooper-mountain-nature-park

Phone: 503-629-6350

Watch the Episode: www.traveloregon.com/walksonwildside

May

5

Yaquina Headland
Is for the Birds!

*A*s the seasons change, surf and sand often seem to merge into a golden, sun-burnished moment along the coast. The rocky headland called Yaquina (pronounced Yuh-QUINN-uh), marked for miles by a towering white sentinel on the central Oregon coastline, is a wonder. Once a lonely outpost above rocky cliffs, Yaquina Headland and Lighthouse are anything but lonely on crisp, clear days as schoolchildren scamper and tourists wander across some of the most accessible tide pools of the area.

Managed by the Bureau of Land Management (BLM), the Yaquina Head Outstanding Natural Area is home to many seabirds and other sea life. Harbor seals lounge on a nearby series of low, rock islands; the mass migration of gray whales can easily be observed; and low tide reveals seaweeds, sea stars, hermit crabs, purple urchins, and anemones in the nearby "marine gardens."

According to Jay Moeller, chief park ranger, the site's geology is the reason it was chosen for a lighthouse station in 1871: "Yaquina Headland is really an ancient lava flow that originated 14 million years ago in eastern Washington and then spread 300 miles to the west before reaching the ocean. Despite a battering by ocean waves, relentless winds, and seasonal rains, the basalt rock refuses to be worn away as quickly as surrounding beaches."

The headland's enduring prominent face made it a natural choice for the lighthouse. Moeller pointed out some of the finer details of the massive, white, conical-shaped light tower starting with the 114 steps in the circular stairway to the top: "The Yaquina Lighthouse is the tallest and second-oldest lighthouse still in operation and provides the headland its most distinguishing feature. But it's what you can't see that's also amazing, for it's actually built of double-walled brick, more than 370,000 of them, for insulation and dampness protection."

Yaquina Head Lighthouse has been a solitary sentinel for sailors at sea since 1871.

The light was equipped then as it is today with a Fresnel lens that was manufactured in Paris in 1868. It was shipped from France to Panama, transported across the isthmus, and then shipped to Oregon. What a journey! With a laugh, Moeller added that Yaquina Head was always a popular tourist attraction: "When it was built in 1873, the 92-foot tower was a skyscraper and so many tourists came to see it that the keepers had to ask the local officials to declare visiting hours. It was the only way they could get their work done and get some sleep."

Chris Burns, a BLM volunteer and historian, explained that a hundred years ago this central coast region was so isolated, especially in winter, that the lightkeepers and their families had to be a very dedicated lot: "The men had a variety of responsibilities, but the main thing was always making sure the light was working. That service was critical above all because there were so many shipwrecks along our rugged coast in those days. The light had to stay on at all costs. It was more important than anything else out here."

Several miles of trail connect visitors to various interpretive sites with kiosks throughout the headland. One trail leads from the interpretive center to an observation deck with a dramatic vista of the ocean and Newport—just 3 miles away. Mother Nature has created something amazing here—a beautiful place where marine creatures can live and humans can easily observe them.

5A Yaquina Headland and Lighthouse

Where: 750 NW Lighthouse Drive, Newport, OR 97365

Web: www.blm.gov/or

Phone: 541-574-3100

Watch the Episode: www.traveloregon.com/yaquinahead

More Coastal Wildlife Stops

Whale Watch Center

*S*ome people go the extra mile to teach you about Oregon's wildlife legacy. Gloria and Alan Koch set up what amounts to an outdoor classroom to teach the people who stop in at Boiler Bay State Scenic Viewpoint. It's a good place for visitors to pause for a lesson and hard to miss because the "Whale Watch Spoken Here" sign rests alongside Coastal Highway 101. "We are here because we love the whales," noted Gloria, who added that she and Alan have been "teachers in residence" as Boiler Bay whale watch volunteers for almost a decade. Gloria added that their stay during whale watch week is a teaching tradition they never miss because, "We are real advocates for the whales . . . and it's only when you understand and appreciate an animal that you will do something to help that animal survive on this earth." It is the size of the gray whales that captures our imaginations. As big as a bus and yet they glide through the water with a smoothness and ease. There is so much to admire about the gray whales' long-distance romance. Consider their journey: it's a round-trip of more than 12,000 miles from the Arctic to Baja birthing grounds and now, in early May, they are swimming back home to the Arctic again.

When the weather is too foul to watch for them outdoors, you can duck indoors at nearby Depoe Bay and learn even more. Morris Grover, manager of Oregon State Park's Whale Watching Center, said it is a gateway to understanding the giants of the deep. He said that thousands of people from all over the world travel to Oregon in the spring just to see the gray whales—hundreds of visitors stop in at the center each week—an unassuming building that is perched just above the ocean breakers in the center of town: "We have artifacts of all sorts: skeletons of seals and sea lions plus short movies about different kinds of whales. The gray whales are actually doing very well—we think there are about 19,000 right now, so it's a very healthy herd. They are one of the great recovery stories since they were removed from the federal endangered species list."

Here's a tip I learned many years ago from one of the whale watch volunteers at the Hatfield Marine Science Center in Newport: try to see the big picture by scanning the ocean with your eyes rather than jumping from one spot to another. If you use your vision like it's set for a wide-screen format, you'll see the blow better than you will by using binoculars to bring the view closer. Also, when talking with others in a group try to find a common language for distance or location so everyone can enjoy the show. There's nothing more frustrating than hearing "I see it!" and you haven't a clue where to look. I use my fingers. That is, when I spy a whale on the sea, I'll raise my hand horizontally to the distant horizon, count the number of finger widths from the horizon down to the whale in the ocean, and then tell others to do the same. It really works!

Back at Boiler Bay, volunteer Alan Koch said that he's been through an incredible training program to teach whale biology, natural history, and the problems the gray giants face in the ocean. "Pollution of our water is number one," said Koch, "whether it's an oil spill, or dumping our garbage in the ocean, it all affects all the animals. Truth is, it affects us too because we eat food from the sea. If we pollute the sea it's going to hurt us." Morris Grover agreed: "People are very concerned about those issues today. The fact that we've got these big animals right in our backyard, and the fact that they've come back from virtual extinction is something visitors appreciate and respect."

5B Boiler Bay State Scenic Viewpoint

Where: Located on Oregon's Central Coast, off US Highway 101,
1 mile north of Depoe Bay

Web: www.oregonstateparks.org

Phone: 541-265-4560 or 800-551-6949

5C Depoe Bay Whale Watching Center

Where: 126 North Coast Highway, Depoe Bay, OR 97341

Web: www.oregonstateparks.org

Phone: 541-765-3304, ext. 3407

Watch the Episode: www.traveloregon.com/oregonwhalewatching

Hatfield Marine Science Center

The Hatfield Marine Science Center is headquarters for scores of professional educators and scientists linked with Oregon State University, but the visitor center illustrates various natural sciences through hands-on demonstrations, kiosks, and larger exhibits. The public aquarium is a window to the ocean for about 300,000 visitors each year. Displays feature marine-related research conducted by Oregon State University's academic programs in fishery biology, management, and aquaculture, as well as in marine biology aspects of tidal, estuarine, and near-shore marine environments. Many displays are interactive and range in scope from global remote sensing down to the microscopic level. You can also enroll in day- or week-long classes that are offered each summer that will let you experience more hands-on science in the field.

5D Hatfield Marine Science Center

Where: 2030 SE Marine Science Drive, Newport, OR 97365
Web: hmsc.oregonstate.edu
Phone: 541-867-0100
Watch the Episode: www.traveloregon.com/marinescience

Sea Lion Caves

Sea Lion Caves is more than 100 acres of ocean shoreline and adjacent land and it has been in private ownership since 1887. It's also been a "drawing card for the curious," said general manager Boomer Wright. He explained that the massive cave is the largest along the West Coast and where 250 Steller sea lions are a raucous, rowdy crowd. "They are very social animals with their barking, crawling over each other, and even nipping one another." Wright added that up to 1,000 Steller sea lions use the cave from November through late summer: "They are often seen lounging, loafing, or just plain sacked out on the rocky interior cliffs or boulders. Of course, there is the large center rock that we call 'King of the Hill,'" noted Wright, "and there is usually a bit of fighting between sea lions to see who gets to rest atop it."

Lounging harbor seals are one of many marine species you will see at Sea Lion Caves.

The Steller sea lions are not the only wildlife species that are easy to spy at Sea Lion Caves. Back atop, keep eyes out for soaring raptors like hawks and eagles that are often seen on the hunt—or flocks of shorebirds that dance and dazzle and skirt the surf. Wright said that it is a remarkable scene and one that is often overlooked in winter: "Without a doubt, it's the most gorgeous stretch of the Oregon coast with the collection of rocky shores, so the geology, the geography, and certainly the forest add up to a wonderful place to relax and wonder and wander if you want a place to decompress."

5E Sea Lion Caves

Where: 91560 US Highway 101, Florence, OR 97439
Web: www.sealioncaves.com
Phone: 541-547-3111
Watch the Episode: www.traveloregon.com/capeperpetua

6

Paddle for
Peace of Mind

*S*ome getaways offer peace of mind with each stroke of a paddle and all you need is a buoyant vessel, a life vest, and a spirit of adventure at the new Beaver Creek State Natural Area near Newport. It is unlike any state parkland you've ever visited.

Beaver Creek has a relatively short run; a mere 30-mile-long stream that is born in the Oregon Coast Range Mountains and enters the ocean at Ona Beach. The complex of state park properties is now called Brian Booth State Park. It was renamed by the Oregon State Parks and Recreation Commission in 2013 to honor the first chairperson of the original commission (1990-97).

Brian Booth State Park is a fine, forested ocean flat that is perfect for extensive daytime shore use. No camping is allowed, but the park offers easy access for beachcombing and large picnic gatherings.

Never head to the great outdoors without binoculars for they make the wildlife viewing more enjoyable.

Retired park manager Mike Rivers and I paddled stable, flat-bottomed kayaks through a stretch of Beaver Creek where the freshwater mixes with the salt. He told me that the creek is never more than 6 feet deep throughout its length, but it does rise and fall a bit with the tidal change. The new state park natural area is nearly 400 acres of freshwater marsh and uplands and a place where the creek's namesake animal—also the Oregon state animal—has made a remarkable come-back over the past 40 years.

Their signs were everywhere, from chewed up alder sticks scattered on shore to large semi-submerged logs where beaver teeth appeared like double chisel-type marks on the wood to several large lodges. "This time of year, the lodges are overgrown with brush and other vegetation," noted Rivers. "They're pretty impossible to see from a distance, but in a kayak you can sneak up and check them out pretty close. It's pretty neat!" In fact, our paddling was highlighted with close-up views of varied birds rarely seen so near at hand and included hawks, eagles, and egrets. Rivers added that the parkland includes 7 miles of boat-accessible hiking trails leading through meadows and forests.

At the top of a nearby knoll, the new Beaver Creek Visitor Center—accessible by land or water—offers maps, photos, and information about the wildlife in the area. Rivers added, "This is really a first for Oregon State Parks and yet there's a demand for this kind of recreation that doesn't really involve any kind of development at all; just a minimum impact, a minimum footprint on the landscape." For folks who wish to make their visit a longer stay, South Beach State Park Campground is just 6 miles away: "At South Beach," noted Rivers, "we often find ourselves as a hub for recreation and overnight stays. We have over 250 campsites—all full-service campsites with electricity and water at each site. We've twenty-seven yurts with electricity, water, and indoor sleeping facilities: a futon couch and bunk bed."

But it's out on the water where you'll likely find me—where nature's touch soothes the soul at an Oregon State Park that is essentially a watery wilderness. "We're thinking of our children and their children who will come here too. This is a fabulous area," said Rivers. Visitors can sign up for guided tours of Beaver Creek State Natural Area at nearby South Beach State Park in Newport. The tours are led by a state park guide and they are offered daily between the Fourth of July and Labor Day but special arrangements for group tours can be made at other times of the year. You can also learn more about Beaver Creek guided tours through the private tour operator, Northwest EcoExcursions in Depoe Bay, Ossies Surf Shop in Newport, and Central Coast Watersports in Florence.

6 Beaver Creek Welcome Center

Where: Located 1 mile east of Ona Beach and US Highway 101
on Beaver Creek Road

Web: www.oregonstateparks.org

Phone: 541-563-6413

Watch the Episode: www.traveloregon.com/beavercreekstatepark

Horsenecks, Quahogs, and Cockles

Shovels and weeding rakes can be a sure sign of spring when gardeners go to work in their yards but the handy-dandy tools don't always have to be used for work. Sometimes, they can also be used for recreation and I guarantee: you will really dig this adventure!

Oregon's springtime super low tides are the best because that's a time when the dinner table is set. Mitch Vance, shellfish biologist with the Oregon Department of Fish and Wildlife (ODFW), said that any of the really good low tides during daylight hours provide ample opportunities to harvest Oregon's varied bay clam species: "Some folks like to get out as early as possible and have more digging opportunity; they follow that tide as it goes out, looking for new exposed areas and then work back as the tide turns to flood."

Norm and Bonnie Clow recently traveled to Tillamook Bay from their home in Dayton, Oregon. They were among the first early risers to explore the exposed sand and gravel bars on a sunrise clamming adventure. The Clows have been digging their dinner on the bay for more than

When you go bay clamming all you need is a bucket, a shovel,. and an Oregon Shellfish License to dig your supper from the sea.

60 years and said the 4 A.M. wake-up call was "no big deal!" Best advice for the novice clam digger? "Keep digging," Norm said with a chuckle. "Usually, the clams are thick enough that if you dig one hole and excavate out, you will have little problem harvesting a limit."

April, May, and June each provide many super low minus tides that occur early in the morning. This is the favored time for digging bay clams with names like horsenecks, quahogs, steamers, and cockles. Jeff Folkema, a local guide and the owner of Garibaldi Marina, showed off a half dozen of the prized horseneck clams that he harvested from the bay. He said they are called "gaper" clams because of the "gape" in the shell where the neck pokes through. "This is a nice size," he said while handling a hefty 2- to 3-pound grapefruit-sized bivalve. "This is pretty average size with a lot of meat. A good-sized clam but I have seen much bigger too."

Folkema added that clam diggers 14 years and older are required to purchase an Oregon Shellfish License, "and remember that each person who is harvesting clams must have their own container—a bucket or a clam net on their belt—even a plastic bread bag will do—because you cannot lump other people's clams into your container—you'll get a ticket for that."

Keep your eyes open for Oregon Department of Fish and Wildlife placards that show pictures of the different clam species along with the harvest limits and other regulations. Vance offered: "If you're digging it really helps to know what you're after so you can understand the regulations around that species." He added that abundant food and reliable cold, clean water contribute to perfect habitat for bay clam populations in most of Oregon's coastal estuaries.

As diggers gathered their clams, ODFW biologists gather information from them on the harvest and the location and quantity of the catch. Vance added, "We are trying to get some really specific location information on which bay clam species are in a single hole—so our surveyors will walk up to a recreation digger, tell them what he's doing, take a GPS point, and then mark what species they're getting from that hole."

The work has been ongoing for 5 years—documenting the clam catch in four Oregon estuaries including Coos Bay, Yaquina Bay, Netarts, and Tillamook Bays. Recently, ODFW revealed remarkable results from their research: New "clam maps" available for free download or in brochure form that show the results of the study.

Biologist Tony D'Andrea said, "We have maps for Garibaldi that show where the four recreationally important clams are—including butters, cockles, gapers, and steamers—it'll tell you where they are found in that particular location. You can find those hot spots for the different clam species that you might be interested in gathering."

There is also a tasty reward for the clam digger's efforts—bay clams can be delicious according to local resident Don Best, who showed off his limit of quahog clams. One of his all-time favorite recipes is an old-fashioned clam fritter: "All it takes is a little cracker crumb, flour, and egg—perhaps some chopped onion. Chop up the clams, mix them with the batter, and fry them in a skillet with oil. They are awesome that way!"

Vance added that in addition to supper from the sea, digging bay clams can provide hours of family fun for each member of the family: "Oh, it is really good for families because it's so easy and there's not a lot of gear—just a shovel or a rake—so get the kids in some boots and get them out here and have some fun in the sand."

Don Best's Clam Frittter Recipe

Vegetable oil, divided	2 eggs
1 cup unsifted flour	½ cup milk
2 teaspoons baking powder	¼ cup reserved clam liquid
½ cup bread crumbs	2 cups finely chopped clams
½ teaspoon salt	

In deep-fat fryer or large, heavy skillet, heat oil to 375°F. Sift together flour, baking powder, bread crumbs, and salt; set aside.

In a medium mixing bowl, beat eggs, milk, reserved clam liquid, and 1 tablespoon oil. Stir in dry ingredients and clams. Drop mixture by heaping tablespoonfuls into hot oil. Fry until golden on all sides. Drain on paper towels. Refrigerate leftovers.

Makes 15 to 18 fritters, serving about 4.

A Hospital for the Wild

*T*hroughout my travels as outdoor reporter the past three decades, few people have impressed me more with their passion and sense of purpose to care for the critters than the kindhearted woman who found her life's calling in the rural countryside near Astoria in Clatsop County. I first journeyed to the Wildlife Center of the North Coast to meet Sharnelle Fee for a special television program in 1998 (following many positive reports I'd heard about her successful wildlife care efforts) only to arrive in the midst of a surprising and terrible spring storm. A pow-

erful cold front aimed straight at Oregon had raced out of the Gulf of Alaska. It was staging a relentless springtime attack on the coastline with 90 miles-per-hour winds building massive, endless breakers that rolled and exploded onto shore. This was a time when nature was at its spectacular roughest, and yet it was against that backdrop of coastal wildness that I found a remarkable back eddy of calm at her small wildlife hospital.

The patients at this hospital are exceptional. "Each year, we have wildlife species that get into trouble," said Fee. "My job is to make them well." I was visiting her facility for a news story that centered on a massive

Sharnelle Fee's helping hands care for hundreds of sick or injured common murres each year.

die-off of common murres along the Oregon coast. Her wildlife hospital cared for more than 1,000 murre chicks that had washed ashore at numerous beaches in Clatsop and Tillamook Counties. The birds were gathered—by hand—by scores of volunteers that Fee enlisted to help. It really was a remarkable scene—the baby birds were everywhere—in cages, pens, small fenced areas across the floor of her hospital—many of the birds were starving and had to be hand-fed small amounts of fish to bring them back to health.

Fee said that her facility usually takes in 2,000 patients each year, but caring for so many murre chicks at one time was a bit overwhelming. Still, that's the nature of Fee's commitment to help wildlife, birds large or small—from murres to cormorants to pelicans—that show up on her doorstep. Fee told me that her mission was "to help the sick or injured critters recover from whatever ails them." I also learned that "raptors and rifles" constitute a common theme at the care center too. In fact, scores of wounded birds are brought to the clinic each year, and Fee is able to patch up many of them for release back to the wild. But for a not-so-lucky few, fate has determined another path. The otherwise healthy birds become ambassadors of sorts for wildlife education programs. As we walked and talked, Fee proudly described her many resident birds, including a mature bald eagle whose right wing was but a mere stub of its former self—another gunshot wound, this one amputated. "The raptors get into trouble by flying into power lines or they are hit by vehicles or sometimes people just shoot them for fun too," said Fee.

All of her assistants are volunteers and the remarkable 2,500-square-foot facility with a 350,000-dollar price tag was paid for by grants and donations. Fee credits the local community and the many people who believe wildlife at risk deserve all the help we can give them. It takes will and determination to care for wildlife. In addition to the hands-on care that she and scores of volunteers provide she also takes many of her critters into classrooms to teach youngsters about wildlife. She tells all who will listen that too many coastal animals are wounded by gunfire, or from oil on the beach, or—increasingly—from being bound up in plastic trash, like six-pack rings, Styrofoam, and fishing line. She visits with groups, especially schoolchildren, whenever and wherever she can in order to spread the message that each day she sees wild animals suffering because they encountered humans. "People are such a difficult species to live with," said Fee, ". . . I want to be more than a consumer—I want to give back to this earth and make up for things that I consumed . . . and make a difference on the planet."

7 Wildlife Center of the North Coast

Where: 89686 State Highway 202, Astoria, OR 97103

Web: coastwildlife.org

Phone: 503-338-0331

Watch the Episode: www.traveloregon.com/wildlifecarecenter

8

South Fork Alsea River National Back Country Byway

*I*t's the size of it all that impresses most on a back road adventure that rises and winds for a daylong getaway. You're on the trail to the mountain called Marys Peak, the highest point on the Oregon Coast Range and it may just steal your heart along the way. It is something special on a day when soggy skies clear and sun beams light up a scene that's filled with so much vibrant color: from crimson paintbrush to brilliant blue larkspur or stunning yellow wallflowers. Many wildflower species are at your side as you explore the lush meadows, dense noble fir forests, and the many hiking trails that link all of it together. In fact, more than 12 miles of trails crisscross Marys Peak, nearly all of them connected to the spacious parking area where many folks begin their adventures. The most popular trail is the mile-long Summit Trail that leads you up a moderate grade. Soon, you're face to face with an amazing scene: a bird's-eye view of the grand Willamette Valley. You easily spy the small town of Philomath—then the larger Corvallis just beyond. Even a hazy day cannot diminish the stunning size of the many Cascade Mountain peaks you can see: Rainier, St. Helens, Adams, Hood, Jefferson, and the Three Sisters are easily picked out against the eastern skyline.

While to the west, Newport's beaches are often seen with the breaking surf line just 26 miles away. It is a glorious view, no doubt about that—but all these high Cascade Mountain peaks may leave you wondering, what about the namesake: Marys Peak. Well, who was Mary? Some anecdotal stories suggest an Indian legend and linkage—for this place had been called a "house or home of spirits" by ancient peoples. Other tales suggest a pioneer lineage a century old or older when white settlers first arrived in Oregon country. There is a nearby town site of Marysville and a nearby Marys River, but the fact is no one really knows and so the history behind the naming of Marys Peak remains a mystery.

Alsea Falls does so in a 40-yard stretch of foamy delight.

It's no secret that the wildflower show draws a real crowd—not just of people, but swarms of butterflies seem to hover just above bloom top across the open meadows each May and June. The fragile insects come in many sizes and colors, but keep an eye out for the larger swallowtail butterfly for it's a favorite and hard to miss. Nor is the summit of Marys Peak with its distinct array of metallic antennas for radio, cell phone, and broadcast television transmissions. Marys Peak stands tall at more than 4,100 feet and that makes the trees, the insects, flowers, and grasses distinct—even rare for the Oregon Coast Range. That alone makes the site worth a visit. Perhaps you'll consider a longer stay. If you packed a tent, sleeping bag, and food, nearby Marys Peak Campground's secluded sites offer an affordable overnight stay. At the least, do bring hiking boots and a camera on this getaway—they will provide you a comfortable and enjoyable way to savor Marys Peak: a unique mountain of dizzying heights and colorful delights.

Let Marys Peak be just the start of a daylong adventure that leads you toward new territory near the small burg of Alpine, Oregon. Continue west and discover a trail marked by spring wildflowers, gorgeous forested scenery, and a spectacular waterfall whose prime time is passing along the South Fork Alsea River National Back Country Byway. Be prepared to spend some time and savor a trail that threads through the heart of the Coast Range Mountains to reach the South Fork Alsea River. It is a roadway so significant that the Bureau of Land Management (BLM) designated 11 miles of it a national back country byway. The river is often by your side and you will slow down to enjoy it for the narrow winding asphalt gives you little choice.

On a gorgeous sunlit day, the small feeder creeks run full across lush moss as wildflowers like trillium and fairy slipper orchids reach their full bloom. Soon, it's time to trade in the truck for two legs at the Alsea Falls Recreation Site that offers nearly 8 miles of hiking trails—including one that skirts the South Fork of the Alsea River—where you can fully appreciate what makes this place so special. One of the features I especially enjoy is Alsea Falls—roaring across ancient basalt rock in a 125-foot stretch that finishes in a foamy moment—that is worth a pause before you move along.

You're apt to find me along this river on a day when sunbeams light up the scene and wildflowers wave you along as the river rolls on to its magical, ageless song. The South Fork Alsea River National Back Country Byway is not to be missed. A couple things to remember: while the BLM opens the Alsea Falls Recreation Site picnic area and campgrounds in mid-May, the hiking trails are open anytime and the South Fork Alsea River National Backcountry Byway is open year-round.

8A Marys Peak

Where: Siuslaw National Forest, off State Highway 34 on Marys Peak Road

Phone: 541-750-7000; Fax: 541-750-7234

Watch the Episode: www.traveloregon.com/maryspeak

8B Alsea River National Back Country Byway

Where: Follow the South Fork Alsea River between the towns of Alsea and Glenbrook.

Web: www.blm.gov/or

Phone: 503-375-5646

Watch the Episode: www.traveloregon.com/alseabyway

June

9

Fernhill Gardens

A community's health can be measured by its wealth of wild places . . . and in western Washington County you can discover what's been a bit of an outdoor secret where the quiet life is prized by its wildness. If you're lucky you may cross paths with wildlife photographer Steve Halpern. He travels this way each week and he takes a deep breath and savors a place that's meant for the quiet times. "In order to do bird photography, you have to have an extraordinary tolerance for frustration," said the longtime photographer. "You have to have high patience, be willing to endure perhaps cold and heat and bugs, and remember that none of that shows up in the picture." What

Fernhill Wetlands is prized for its varied wildlife, including the solitary blue heron.

does show up in Halpern's wonderful bird photographs are moments of wildness that are set in a place you've likely never seen or heard much about called Fernhill Wetlands near Forest Grove, Oregon. "Part of it is learning bird behavior so you can get close without startling the bird. You can get a nice picture of the subject in its natural habitat without it being alarmed."

You may find it surprising that so much wildness—nearly 800 acres—is just 30 minutes west of Portland. Once considered a "wasteland," the local community thought there had to be a better way and began to change the scene over 20 years ago. The restoration and preservation efforts paid off—today, it's a place where eagles have a home and raise their young and where thousands of waterfowl gather each winter. Halpern calls Fernhill Wetlands a "birder's paradise" and it's largely unknown: "I think it's an amazing thing, not just for the wildlife, but for the city of Forest Grove and for Washington County to have a world-class wetland. This is as good and as wonderful a wetland as you could hope for and it's really in our own backyards." Recently, that fine place just off our backyards got even better. The landowner, Clean Water Services, embarked on a 5-year, 18-million-dollar project that runs through 2017 to enhance the Fernhill Wetlands property with a more natural system of cleaning wastewater. Three acres of the property—and there's much more underway—have been transformed into Fernhill Gardens, a site marked by massive boulders, huge trees, and nearly 60,000 wetland shrubs and plants. The practical goal of the project is to cool treated wastewater at an affordable price before it flows into the nearby Tualatin River.

Project manager John Dummer said that a project of this scale has never been built before: "The process of naturalizing or bringing water back to nature is one of the things we wanted to evoke in this restorative garden. We want this to be a place where people can come experience nature but also provide a purpose of cleaning and cooling the water; hence, all of the vegetation." The garden is a place that people will certainly want to visit—crowned by two massive wooden bridges that invite and entice visitors down the trail. Water Resources Manager Jared Kinnear added, "It's a win-win for the water, win-win for the habitat and really, offers amenities for the people too." Local people like Debby de Carlo (a member of the local Friends of Fernhill Wetlands) agreed that the new garden will be a valuable asset to the community and to the wildlife that live here. "This place is like a silver lining of Oregon's rainy winters," said de Carlo. "You see more variety of ducks here in the winter and when I'm out in a natural place like this, I forget about myself. It's almost like a meditation to be out here surrounded by wildness." Halpern agreed and said that as folks discover Fernhill, more people will come to appreciate what it offers: "It's a place where our national bird has successfully come back from the brink of extinction. That's really a remarkable thing and it's good to know there's still something wild out here."

9A Fernhill Wetlands

Where: 1399 SW Fern Hill Road, Forest Grove, OR 97117
Web: www.fernhillnts.org
Phone: 503-992-3200
Watch the Episode: www.traveloregon.com/fernhillgardens

Just for the Kids

F amilies who like to ramble, explore, and generally hang out in Oregon's forests may wish to visit two sites that bring out the adventurer in each of us—but you should know: these getaways are for kids . . . of any age. To start, test your climbing skills in a forested parkland where you'll experience a bird's-eye view to the woods. It's a vantage point that will take your breath away: up to 60 feet off the ground!

It is found only at the unique Tree to Tree Aerial Adventure Park set in the foothills of the Oregon Coast Range in western Washington County. The 57-acre forested parkland is unlike anything you've ever experienced off the ground. In fact, you might consider it a playground in the trees. Instructor Patrick Murphy guides folks across the four different tree-to-tree courses—each course is progressively more challenging and he helps people find steady steps on a shaky trail or across a swinging, swaying wobbly way. Murphy said, "This is something that kids like to do—they like to come out and be active, climb in the trees—use their imaginations—pretend to be monkeys or Tarzan or whatever . . . all sorts of fun stuff built for young and old to play up in the trees."

Each climber must wear a safety harness that connects with two lanyards that sport lobster claw–type clips that link you to thick wire cables. Each cable can hold up to 10,000 pounds, so once you're clipped in—you're not going anywhere except across the aerial trail.

The Tree to Tree Park is a family-owned business, according to co-owner Molly Beres. She said the park's location (a short drive from Scoggins Valley Park and Henry Hagg Lake) has attracted a following once visitors discovered their park's unique features. "Portland is the best place for this sort of thing because there are so many outdoorsy people here. Everyone likes to be outside doing active things and extreme sports and this will fit in just fine."

The park also offers a course for the littlest of climbers with the same elements as the adult version but it is much closer to the ground. The course admission isn't based on age—but on height—that is, with your arms extended overhead you must be able to reach 6 feet, 6 inches to play on the full-sized course after you've passed the Basic Training Course. If a youngster is unable to reach 6 feet, 6 inches but can reach at least 5 feet with their arms extended, he or she can play on the smaller course.

The park's many course features are called "elements" and range from simple swaying bridges to horizontal rock walls and tunnels that you must climb across or climb through so to continue the course. Many participants agreed that the climbing experience felt safe despite the 50-foot elevation and that it is an experience full of surprises. First-timer Pete Conklin noted, "It definitely tests your balance and your fear of heights— makes you a little nervous—but all of it is doable."

That feeling never lets up on the course either—it's surpassed only by the thrilling payoff that waits for each climber at the end. "We end every course with a zip line and so it's the payoff for your hard work because everybody loves a zip," noted a smiling Beres. "Our whole purpose is to be outdoors, enjoy nature, and enjoy being in Oregon—just to love where you are—it's the best!"

Another great kid-centric destination is Silver Falls State Park's "Nature Play Area," and after you visit you may wonder: how is it I've not been here before? "One of the things we see happening is kids coming over here and building forts," said Oregon State Parks Manager Steve Janiszewski. "That's OK! We want to see that. We want their parents to come out here and play with their kids too."

The park has installed the new natural play area designed with play "pods" mimicking the habitats of native animals. At each pod, marked with a colorful jumbo-sized totem pole, kids can experience what it's like to be a bear clambering into a log den, a bird shaping a nest out of twigs, or a cougar tracking a deer through the forest.

Stuart Rue and Sarah Evan brought their two young boys, Archer and Anders, to explore the play area and they had a blast! The purpose of the play area is to get kids outside and engaged with nature, as well as to spur creativity and promote a better understanding of animal capabilities and interactions between species. "It's got a nice blend of the traditional play elements with the nature elements and I like that," said Evans. "We try to do a lot with our kids outdoors and we love to go camping, hiking. We all love being outside."

Silver Falls State Park's "Nature Play Area" is the first of its kind in an Oregon state park and so more are planned in the future.

9B Tree to Tree Aerial Adventure Park

Where: 2975 SW Nelson Road, Gaston, OR 97119

Web: www.treetotreeadventurepark.com

Phone: 503-357-0109

9C Silver Falls State Park Natural Play Area

Where: Located on State Highway 214, 26 miles east of Salem. The Nature Play Area is at the north end of the park.

Web: www.oregonstateparks.org

Phone: 503-873-8681, ext. 31

Watch the Episode: www.traveloregon.com/treetotree

10

Youth Outdoor Day

*A*s summer kicks into high gear, plan on some valuable lessons that will boost your kid's confidence for camping, fishing, exploring, and dozens of other activities at the Oregon Fish and Wildlife Department's one-stop outdoor shopping affair for youngsters and their parents. Nearly 800 youngsters discover that learning about the outdoors is fun when the lessons are filled with hands-on opportunities at a unique Youth Outdoor Day at the E. E. Wilson Wildlife Area near Corvallis. "It is the largest outdoor fair of its kind," said Youth Outdoor Day cochair Steve Sessa. He added, "No one is by a TV, in front of a computer, and there's no one texting right now. Everyone is engaged in the outdoors and that's just great."

Small fry can learn how to catch big fish on Youth Outdoor Day.

The daylong annual event offers thirty-five different outdoor recreation activities for youngsters who learn by doing from instructors who've donated their time and materials. The instructors bring their skills while twenty-five organizations provide the equipment and assorted gear so that young people can see and feel what it's like to shoot a shotgun, handle a bow and arrow, create a piece of wildlife art, or send out a champion dog on a long-distance retrieve.

Most kids like Morgan Frederick and her sister Sydney had never done anything like it before: "I got over the fear of shooting a shotgun," said a beaming Morgan. "It doesn't hurt my shoulder because I learned how to hold it the right way. Everyone's helpful and offers advice if you need it." "It really is fun," added

Sydney. "If a kid is outdoorsy at all, they might want to come here and learn a lot more things about the outdoors."

The Oregon Department of Fish and Wildlife (ODFW) staff spends days preparing the E. E. Wilson Wildlife Area to handle the crowds and provide plenty of parking for folks who traveled from throughout Oregon to attend. Scores of staff also volunteer for the agency's flagship event. In fact, more than 250 volunteers offer their time and expertise each year. "People are just clamoring to get outdoors with their families," said ODFW spokesperson Chris Willard. "Even though it's billed as a youth event, what you see out here are families engaged in the outdoors and discovering what varied activities mean to them. We hope to show families how easy it is to bond through outdoor activities."

Valerie Duncan said the event was spot-on as a way to engage her three youngsters: "A great place for kids to learn about conservation. We've seen reptile displays, dog training, even archery and a lot of activities that we'd never find anywhere else. We're excited to be here and excited to learn more and the atmosphere's wonderful."

The Oregon State Marine Board, Oregon Hunters Association, Association of Northwest Steelheaders, the NRA, Ducks Unlimited, and the Oregon Wildlife Heritage Foundation are just some of the groups that help the state fish and wildlife agency put on the affair. It is a remarkable event—even more so because the organizers do little to advertise Youth Outdoor Day. They'd rather spend their dollars on developing more children's activities than marketing. The spring event is really just the start. There are many other ODFW workshops for kids and their families that continue year-round.

---

10 E. E. Wilson Wildlife Area

Where: 29555 Camp Adair Road, Monmouth, OR 97361
Web: www.dfw.state.or.us
Phone: 541-745-5334
Watch the Episode: www.traveloregon.com/youthoutdoorday

11

Gobble, Gobble, Gobble

A number of years ago, I was invited to observe and document one of the most amazing wildlife capture-transplant projects that I'd ever seen: a wild turkey roundup. It seemed too many wild turkeys had taken over a Douglas County homeowner's backyard—more than 100 of the large birds had gathered around the home. They roosted in the surrounding trees, on the roof of the home, strutted across the home's wooden deck and the spacious backyard—the flock had become a nuisance and the homeowner had had enough of their droppings

The male turkey is called a "Tom" and sports a brilliant red snood that grows over its beak and down its head.

A group of turkeys is called a "rafter" and can gather in numbers as high as 100.

and their incessant noisy calls—in fact, many of the large male birds or "Toms" tipped the scales at 20 pounds and had become quite aggressive toward people during the spring breeding season, sometimes even chasing the homeowner's kids across the yard.

Oregon Department of Fish and Wildlife Biologist Steve Denney told me that the flock hadn't always been so large, but through the years the birds discovered that it was a safe environment and the food was reliable and good. "It is usually a big mistake to feed turkeys," said Denney. "They will go from wild birds to half tame very fast if they have a regular food offering." In this case, the homeowner had been tossing out handfuls of cracked corn—thinking the birds need a "little extra" to get them through the winter months. Denney added, "Turkeys will eat almost anything and they are perfectly capable of surviving in wonderful shape throughout the winter without the cracked corn."

Oregon's turkey population is an example of a successful wildlife introduction program—the birds first arrived in Oregon as a part of an exchange program with wildlife managers in other states. Denney explained that wild turkeys are not native to Oregon and that two turkey subspecies have been introduced to Oregon. The Merriam's wild turkey was the first subspecies released in Oregon in 1961.

Live-trapped Merriam's turkeys were brought to Oregon from Colorado, Arizona, New Mexico, Nebraska, and Montana. Since then, more than 10,000 turkeys have been transplanted to locations all over Oregon; initial populations were released in the Douglas County area and also Wasco County in the Columbia River Gorge. The Rio Grande wild turkey was introduced to southwestern Oregon in 1975. Rio Grande turkeys are native to riparian (streamside) zones and scrub woodlands from the southern Great Plains southward into northeastern Mexico.

Still, the good life for turkeys had taken a toll on the frustrated homeowner who thought he had done a good deed, but then realized too late that he'd created a wildlife dilemma. Denney decided upon a unique action plan: he and a small team of technicians rigged a large fabric mesh net with three small rockets—the rockets would launch the net over a baited site to capture as many birds as possible.

We gathered the evening prior to "launch" to determine the best location for the net, the team, and the best observation spot for my photographer. Seven hours later we collected our gear and sat in the dim light of a spring sunrise. I positioned myself next to Denney so to watch the events unfold—he had a radio in one hand and the other was poised over the electronic trigger that would set off the rockets—an observer was hidden in a brush line adjacent to the net and rockets—he patiently waited until most of the birds were inside the net's perimeter. (Cracked corn had been spread across the net to attract the flock.)

At just the right moment the observer gave Denney a radio "flash" signal and then I heard "Three, two, one—Lift off!" as the biologist flipped a switch on the remote control. The three rockets ignited with flames of red and yellow and "whooshed" in an arc over the flock of birds—trailing the large net behind. It

Wild turkeys are highly adaptable and can be seen in every region of Oregon.

was a remarkable sight as leaves and feathers flew from more than thirty turkeys that rushed to escape the net. The small team of "turkey wranglers" hurried in and began the process of capturing the birds—one at a time—taking great care not to injure any of the large gobblers.

Each turkey was placed in a large cardboard box and they were stacked atop each other in a nearby shed. Over the next couple of hours each bird was weighed, measured, leg-banded—(the band indicated a date and location of their capture), and then re-boxed and placed aboard a trailer for transport to their new homes. We traveled with the team to a rural site in Benton County and watched as the boxes of turkeys were placed next to each other and then opened, allowing the birds to escape into their new habitat of coastal rain forest. As a result of the successful project, the homeowner found some relief and he promised never to feed the wild birds again.

You stand a good chance of finding wild turkeys in every corner of Oregon—from the high desert through the Cascades, across the Willamette Valley, and along the coast. They are highly adaptive, and once they grow to adults, they are nearly predator-free. Your best opportunities to see them include William L. Finley National Wildlife Refuge in Benton County, the Jewell Meadows Wildlife Area in Clatsop County, and Cove Palisades State Park near Madras—each of these locations has proven reliable for spotting wild turkeys. During the winter, turkeys congregate in large flocks, often providing viewing or photography opportunities. During the spring, gobblers exhibit a magnificent breeding display and may be observed and/or photographed by patient individuals who learn proficient use of the hen call to lure birds within camera range.

11A William L. Finley National Wildlife Refuge

Where: 26208 Finley Refuge Road, Corvallis, OR 97333
Web: www.fws.gov
Phone: 541-757-7236

11B Jewell Meadows Wildlife Area

Where: 79878 State Highway 202, Seaside, OR 97138
Phone: 503-755-2264

11C Cove Palisades State Park

Where: 7300 SW Jordan Road, Culver, OR 97734
Web: www.oregonstateparks.org
Phone: 541-546-3412 or 800-551-6949

12

Wild Owyhee Country

*R*ivers are liquid highways that, like their asphalt cousins, course through densely populated cities or remote and sparsely inhabited areas. A few years ago, I found myself on one of the most remote watery byways in Oregon, the Owyhee River. It runs through a corner of the state known as "I-O-N" country because of its close proximity to the state borders of Idaho, Oregon, and Nevada, which mesh together in a vastness covering more than 10,000 square miles. Yet, if you mention the Owyhee to most folks, they stare back at you a tad bewildered and ask, "Did you say Ow-ya-hoo-ee? Or, Aw-ya-hay?" Well, it's pronounced "O-WAA-he," as in "Hawaii." The story goes that Peter Skene Ogden, who led a contingent of Hudson's Bay trappers into the region in 1819, named the Owyhee River. Two Hawaiians had been sent to trap for furs on a tributary of the Snake River, where Ogden was camped. The trappers were killed by Indians, and Ogden named the tributary for them. Over the centuries, the "Hawaii River" name has been corrupted into the "Owyhee River."

Out of the way? It certainly is. This is a most secluded and pristine river, and with the sound of its water rushing through boulder-strewn rapids, it's just the kind of territory that stirs my senses and satisfies my soul. It's where I went looking for adventure with Gerald Moore, who owned and operated Water Otters. We were slated to float the wild Owyhee over 4 days to produce a special outdoor program, and we joined Moore's outfitting and guide company because it specialized in Oregon's hard-to-reach rivers. Also, unlike large white-water rafts that seat up to six people, Water Otters (as the name implies) offered a flotilla of small, more intimate, inflatable kayaks.

Moore floated his first river in 1948 and had been hooked ever since, and told me as much at our launch point near Rome, Oregon, where we gathered to sort out

The towering cliffs of the remote Owyhee River Canyon make you feel small—even tiny.

plans, stow our gear, and prepare for the early June adventure. "The river runs brim-full only in spring when the upstream snowmelt fills the Owyhee River canyon," he explained. "So the river's height depends upon snowpack, and you never know just how big it'll be. Naturally, your beginners are somewhere between apprehensive and scared as hell." He laughed and I chuckled and my photographer looked pensive. Moore proceeded with the loading and the lessons without missing a beat.

"Not to worry, though. This winter was a mild one, so most of the snow melted long ago, and the water's actually low. You'll love it. After the first day, you'll get the feel of things. Stick like glue to our guides and mimic their strokes. That's the quickest way to teach someone how to float a river in these boats. If you feel uncomfortable, you can walk around a rapid and we'll take the boat through for you." This sounded like my kind of voyage, but not so my uncertain partner, Curtis Miller, a longtime news-hound and a premier photographer. He, like many, was a fellow who hadn't spent much time in the far reaches of the high desert where rattlesnakes and scorpions can be everyday encounters.

The Owyhee River country may be considered a forgotten corner of the West, where distances are great and people are few, yet it's also a landscape marked by beautiful, far-flung ranges of sage and tall grass and, just beyond, broken buttes and jagged canyons. A sprawling area, unmatched for its gigantic spectacles, it's little wonder this place has been termed Oregon's Grand Canyon for its multicolored spires, dramatic canyons, sculpted grottoes, natural hot springs, and thrilling rapids. In 1984, Congress designated 120 miles of the Owyhee River, from the Oregon-Idaho border to the Owyhee Reservoir, as "wild" and included it in the National Wild and Scenic Rivers System. The Lower Owyhee may be wild, but not for its enormous, frothy, churning white water. Rather, we left Rome (marked by an ancient, colossal rock wall formation that's appropriately named the "Pillars of Rome"), and our 67-mile downriver adventure to the Lake Owyhee State Park was dominated by friendly rapids, extraordinary scenery, and all-embracing solitude.

The Owyhee River is what river runners call "classic pool and drop," with long stretches of calm, glassy water broken by short bursts of cascading white water. For miles, the river winds and curls like a coiled spring, sometimes in the shade of steep-walled canyons, where freshwater springs seep down the vertical walls. Yet other springs are too hot to sit in unless you cool the water with buckets of icy river water. Then there are petroglyphs chipped by ancient natives into flat-faced basalt blocks, and also petrified trees with stumps frozen into rock.

The inflatable kayaks are a blast. Rapids with names like Artillery and Widow Maker hint of danger and demand a boater's respect. Artillery Rapids, a rolling riot of standing waves, make you feel like a kid on a roller coaster at the county fair. Widow Maker and other rapids are more technical and require some accurate alignment and hard paddling to get through safely. At Montgomery Rapid, the largest rapid on the Owyhee River, I paddled a passage and flew through a water-soaking hole. I flew out of my boat, too, and was very happy I was wearing my life vest—gear that I kept on throughout the river trip.

The payoff for the effort required to travel into the Owyhee River canyon is an escape from the hurried, harried hubbub of city life. That's something I really noticed our second night out when we camped across a wide apron of sand that gently kissed the river. I could feel the quiet shout at me! Surrounded by steep rock towers, I was restless and couldn't sleep. As I gazed up from my snug sleeping bag, I was stunned by a sky stuffed with stars. Moore heard me stir and whispered across our otherwise quiet group of drowsy fellow travelers: "Magnificent, eh Grant? This float combines so much into one trip—you're rafting, you have white water, the fishing, and especially the wildlife. It is the reason I come here." In the dark I imagined his hand sweeping across the night sky to touch the stars: "Almost a religious feeling as though you're closer to God and closer to nature. Virtually everyone I bring into this canyon feels the same way."

The final stretch is a transition—marked by miles of flat water. We tied our boats together, and an outboard motor—hauled for this reason—gave us the extra power to move across 13 miles of Lake Owyhee to the Leslie Gulch take-out. From there a gravel road returned us to civilization and home—and time for reflection. The Owyhee River owns a rhythm of its own, and once people discover it, they become unplugged from the pace and race of their daily lives.

12 Lake Owyhee State Park

Where: 1298 Lake Owyhee Dam Road, Adrian, OR 97901
Web: www.oregonstateparks.org
Phone: 541-339-2331

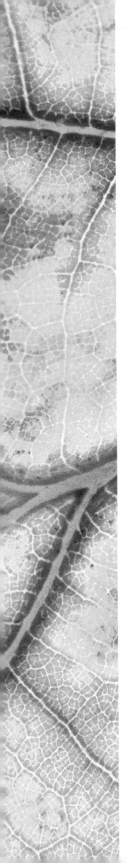

Grant McOmie's Outdoor Talk—
A Wildlife Dilemma

*T*here's no room for mistakes when you land at "Bird Island"—(nicknamed by the scientists who work there) because the tides and the weather don't leave much choice. But under a sun-kissed sky and with a gentle breeze at our backs, we safely arrived ashore at Bird Island. It's a nickname for East Sand Island and it is located just outside the protected harbor of Chinook, Washington, on the lower Columbia River. Photographer Kurt Austin and I joined Oregon State University wildlife researchers who had spent up to 14 hours a day documenting the birds that came to the island to nest, breed, or roost each spring. Tim Marcella and Lauren Reinalda led us through dense brush to reach the island's northern shoreline—from there it was a mile-long hike to reach the first of two stops for armchair views of seabirds that call the island home. We spied the first colony from inside the cover of a wooden blind: the world's largest Caspian tern colony.

Marcella said up to 18,000 terns use the open plot of sand where the female terns scratch out the sand to create nests and then lay their eggs. The tern colony was moved to East Sand Island a decade ago—on purpose. They had overstayed their welcome upriver at Rice Island because

East Sand Island is home to the largest colony of Caspian terns with nearly 20,000 birds.

they ate too many baby salmon there. They eat salmon here too—but only half as many. "The terns eat roughly 8 million baby salmon called 'smolts' each spring," noted Marcella. "That's because East Sand Island is closer to the mouth of the Columbia River and there is a greater abundance and diversity of smaller food fish available for the birds to eat."

Caspian terns aren't alone on Bird Island. Gulls and pelicans weave above the sand and bald eagles are ever watchful for the chance to pounce on easy prey. Reinalda explained why so many birds are drawn to the island: "Well, first, people are not allowed here, except for the research team, so that lack of human contact is big. Plus, islands are very popular for colonial nesting birds because they're isolated from other mammalian predators like foxes and coyotes. Islands are also places where the birds can congregate together, so there's safety in numbers."

The numbers got even bigger down the beach at the opposite end of the island where we crouched down to enter near darkness inside the longest pup tent–like tunnel I had ever seen. It was a 150-yard crawl on hands and knees inside the small fabric tunnel to reach the center of a massive bird colony. We soon found ourselves in a view blind located smack in the middle of the largest cormorant colony in the world. I felt a bit like a gopher or mole as I slowly crawled inside the tunnel and I could hear and smell and see thousands of birds through the fabric—the cormorants are just an arm's length away. Two species, double-crested cormorants and Brandt's cormorants, began showing up to breed and nest on Bird Island just a few years ago. Reinalda suggested that the cormorants had followed the terns to the island and established their colony. Up to 30,000 cormorants have built nests, laid eggs, and raised young in recent years. The cormorants also eat fish. In fact, they eat up to five times more fish than the terns.

Reinalda explained: "Part of our research is to identify more alternatives so that we can provide the managers a suite of options if they decide to manage this bird population." Those options could include killing the salmon-eating cormorants or destroying their nests and eggs, or moving birds to other locations. For now, those decisions are down the road. In the meantime, there will be more scientific research on Bird Island. "Summer nesting and breeding time is a stressful period for terns and cormorants," noted Reinalda. "It is competitive and the search for food is never-ending, especially after the eggs hatch and parents provide for their young. Nesting time is also the purpose of their lives: to continue their species. For us, it's a great opportunity to watch, monitor, and document their nesting successes and failures. It's important for us to understand the bird's life cycles along the Columbia River and the impacts their lives have on our salmon populations."

While East Sand Island is off-limits to visitors, you can experience some of the finest coastal bird viewing across the broad Columbia River inside Fort Stevens State Park. The site is called South Jetty View Tower and it overlooks the south jetty on the Columbia River. Do not hike out on the jetty when the tide is high or during times of high surf. It is extremely difficult negotiating the large boulders that make up the jetty. Besides being slick and difficult to walk across, a sneaker wave can easily wipe you out. Sneaker waves can and do kill a number of people on the Oregon coast who ignore warnings to venture out where it is not safe. The viewing tower rises 20 feet above Parking Lot C and it is a fine place to look for shearwaters, black-legged kittiwakes, scoters, loons, red-necked and western grebes, and many species of gull. This area also is productive for resting migrant birds and will sometimes harbor a snowy or short-eared owl.

Continue driving on Jetty Road as the road curves around the end of the spit and travels east, pull over and hike one of several trails that give a view of the Columbia River. At the end of Jetty Road is a large parking area called Parking Lot D, and at the east end of the parking lot there is a trail that heads south to reach Trestle Bay. It is a prime place for birding with shelter for birders. Inside the "birder's bunker" is a photo poster from which you can identify many of the birds by name. Of course, summer weekends might not be the best time to spot the birds as many people and their dogs enjoy walking along the beaches and tend to scatter the bird life, but this area has produced some good rare birds and offers a view of both sides of the bay.

Postscript: December 2014

This past summer, the US Army Corps of Engineers (ACE) announced plans to kill 16,000 double-crested cormorants on East Sand Island over a period of 4 years. ACE also proposes to remove enough sand to inundate the nesting area of the cormorants, so that birds that leave won't return. The goal is to reduce the double-crested cormorant population on the island to about 5,600 breeding pairs.

Starting in the spring of 2015, ACE proposes to shoot more than half of the iridescent black birds, on the grounds that they're eating too many fish. Besides being commercially valuable, some baby salmon and steelhead that pass through the Lower Columbia River to the ocean are on the Endangered Species List, and that's what is forcing the Army Corps of Engineers to act. The corps owns and manages East Sand Island; indeed, it created the bird colony when it expanded the island with dredging spoils back in the 1980s.

In November, the American Bird Conservancy (ABC), a leading national bird conservation organization, raised multiple objections to assertions by the US Army Corps of Engineers in their proposal to kill 16,000 cormorant birds on East Sand Island (ESI), in the Columbia River Estuary, as part of a plan to reduce predation of juvenile salmonids including salmon smolt by the birds.

ABC asserts that the lethal approach being recommended by the Corps in reducing the numbers of double-breasted cormorants is offered ". . . without adequate justification and explanation of why the same result cannot be achieved through non-lethal methods." ABC says that the expected benefits to salmon hinge not in how cormorant numbers are controlled (through harassment or lethal control), but in the habitat modification that must occur to maintain the breeding double-crested cormorants' population at the Corps' target of 5,600 breeding pairs.

As of this writing, the US Army Corps of Engineers is currently working with the US Fish and Wildlife Service, US Department of Agriculture, Oregon Department of Fish and Wildlife, and the Washington Department of Fish and Wildlife to come up with a plan to lower the cormorant population—or at least mitigate the number of fish they eat.

FS Fort Stevens State Park

Where: 100 Peter Iredale Road, Hammond, OR 97121

Phone: 503-861-1671 or 503-861-3170, ext. 21

July

13

Christmas for Coho

The holiday spirit is shared year-round by a group of enthusiastic anglers who give back to Mother Nature through an ambitious project that is restoring salmon habitat in Clatsop County's Necanicum River. It's an event that has proved that there are many opportunities to "walk the talk" of helping salmon in Oregon. A sportfishing conservation group called Trout Unlimited recently teamed up with local landowner Byren Thompson. The group was moved into action to make a difference for fish by giving their time and money to help nature. For the past three summers, Thompson has created his Coho Sanctuary along a 10-acre stretch of riverside property in Clatsop County through a series of riparian improvement projects—Thompson's Coho Sanctuary is open to visitors who want to see and learn more about what it takes to help salmon survive.

Trout Unlimited collects used Christmas trees that help to create new fish habitat.

The environmental project begins each December and January when Trout Unlimited volunteers collect hundreds of postholiday Christmas trees that are delivered to Thompson's Coho Sanctuary. Each July, the volunteers gather at Thompson's property to create a tree corral of sorts along a bend of the Necanicum River. Remarkably, the Christmas trees have retained most of their needles. Several hundred trees are bundled up and then floated into place and tied off onshore to prevent them from floating down the river. The trees provide critical habitat for baby salmon that are migrating to the sea. They also create shade that cools the water, provide cover for fish to

Nearly 1,000 trees are collected and corralled in the Necanicum River to create shade and cover for baby fish.

escape predators (especially birds), and attract plenty of bugs that are ideal fish food. Local ecologist and environmental consultant Doug Ray said that the used trees—many destined for landfills—find a second life by helping nature: "When we throw this wood in the river and collect them in this short, 40-yard stretch, the fish respond to it within minutes. It's like they are hardwired, genetically, to find and use the cover."

Thompson's Coho Sanctuary was originally designed and developed by his dad, Herb Thompson. Herb realized that he could help more baby salmon survive their journey to the sea by creating more fish habitat on his property. "He had a burning desire to help fish and there would be no stopping him," said Byren's mother, Susan Thompson. "Herb would not take 'no' for an answer and he envisioned that our property would become an educational center, an outdoor classroom with tours and classes to teach people how they can do this on their own lands. Well, it has become what Herb envisioned thanks to all the volunteers and my son, Byren, who continues to lead the fish habitat improvement projects."

Herb Thompson was killed in a logging accident in 2012, but Byren said his dad really believed it was important to give back to nature. "We had always been outdoorsmen and loved to catch fish and Dad thought it was important to help raise more fish by improving the habitat they need. Now, I just enjoy sharing ideas and encouraging other people who visit our center to help fish too. I actually enjoy seeing more fish come back as adult salmon from the efforts that we take now." More volunteers are giving their time to the Coho Sanctuary too. Each January, scores of members from the Tualatin Valley Chapter of Trout Unlimited gather in Lake Oswego to collect hundreds of trees from folks who also donate 10 dollars a tree to help pay the transportation cost of getting the trees from the city to the country. "These trees are instant habitat for baby salmon," said Trout Unlimited member Jeff Price. "Even one tree makes a difference because we've seen dozens of fish come to an area right after we placed a tree in the water. It's amazing to see that kind of biology in action."

Trout Unlimited's Christmas for Coho project made national news when *Field and Stream* magazine awarded the Tualatin Chapter their "Hero for a Day" award that recognized their volunteerism to help salmon. *Field and Stream* even produced a video about the unique project. "We spotlight people who do volunteer efforts to help fish and wildlife habitats," said *Field and Stream* editor, Bob Marshall. "If we give people attention for the good they are doing, it will inspire others to do the same thing."

Back along the Necanicum River, the Coho Sanctuary soon filled with 800 Christmas trees and Thompson noted that by September, thousands of baby salmon gather underwater in the shelter of the trees. "When the first big rain hits in September," said Thompson, "I come down here and cut the line that holds all of these trees in place and they all flush out to the estuary. Next summer, we'll start the project all over again. It really works well." Ray added, "This project is an incredible testament to Herb's vision to find a way, on his own land and with his own time and energy, to give back to nature and then provide opportunities to others, like us, to help too."

"We are just average, everyday people," noted Susan Thompson. "Now we have other organizations getting on board too. All these volunteers who help us— we feel truly blessed to have them so the Coho Sanctuary dream continues. It's a dream measured by a spirit of giving—a Christmas for Coho that lasts all year long."

13 Coho Sanctuary

Where: 33969 US Highway 26, Seaside, OR 97138
Web: cohosanctuary.org
Phone: 503-440-0275

Oregon Council Trout Unlimited

Where: 227 Southwest Pine Street, #200, Portland, OR 97204
Web: www.tuoregon.org
Phone: 503-827-5700

Watch the Episode: www.traveloregon.com/treesforcoho

14

Flying Trout

*E*arly morning—when air is cool and scenery quiet, stunning snow-capped Mt. Hood is a marvel. But for one week every other summer, the silence in Oregon's Cascade Range is broken when a Bell UH-1H helicopter, owned and operated by Columbia Basin Helicopters of La Grande, takes flight with a load of "flying trout." "We start our trout stocking at the Oregon-Washington border and end at the California-Oregon border and we do the entire Pacific Crest Trail from one end of the state to the other," noted state fishery biologist Kurt Cundiff. "It's a pretty awesome view—we get to see a lot of different lakes and areas that most folks just don't visit."

The time is right in summer for outdoor adventure in Oregon's alpine lake regions and if you go, be sure that you take a rod and reel to catch feisty trout. Oregon's high Cascade areas are remote and difficult to reach—usually by horse or on foot, so Oregon Department of Fish and Wildlife's (ODFW) aerial stocking program delivers tens of thousands of the so called "flying trout" on time and on target into nearly 400 high lakes—in one week. Chief pilot Dave McCarty logs more than 22,000 hours in the chopper and said that he wouldn't trade the weeklong adventure for any other job. "I love this job! I see the entire Cascades in one week and it is just amazing! I approach each lake by looking it over first, seeing which way the riffles are blowing on the water. [This helps determine which way the wind is blowing.] If you get turbulence or downdraft you can feel it dragging you a bit, but for the most part it flies real nice."

McCarty pilots up to four flights a day during the weeklong project and had ground support crews scurrying into action on his return to the base. This week's base for the Northern Cascade flights was the Mt. Hood Meadows Ski Area's Sunrise Lodge parking lot. On the ground, tens of thousands of baby rainbow, cutthroat, and brook trout are loaded aboard a special unit called the Aerial Stocking Device, or ASD. ODFW engineers built the fish-hauling unit back in 1997. Ground crews load up to 400 of the 3-inch-long trout into each of thirty aerated tanks on the remote-controlled device. The device sports a rear tailfin and an aerodynamic nose that lend a familiar look—like a miniature space shuttle.

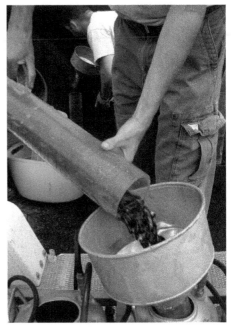

The history of Oregon alpine-lake trout stocking is rich and colorful. In the early days of the twentieth century, horse pack trains made long, arduous treks into the Cascades to deliver the baby fish—it was a summerlong effort to reach all of the lakes that were often frozen over or closed due to slides. In the 1960s, fixed-wing aircraft took over and then helicopters cut down on time and expense. Today, the helicopter with its remote-controlled unit hanging 60 feet under the ship's belly will fly into nearly 400 lakes in just one week.

Fingerling trout are loaded into special tanks for air delivery to mountain lakes.

"The navigator has a list of the lakes that identifies which fish species go into which water body," noted Cundiff. "The navigator gives that information to the bombardier who sits behind him. When McCarty says 'go ahead and release fish,' the bombardier presses a button on the remote controller. That will release the appropriate compartment on the device that holds the fish. It runs real smooth." State fishery biologist Erik Moberly said that the fish do well in Oregon's high lakes but in some years, not all lakes will be stocked. "That's because a lingering winter finds most lakes above 6,000 feet still frozen over so they'll have to wait until next time—that's two years from now."

The baby trout thrive and grow fast in the nutrient-rich lakes—they will grow to catchable size in just one year. A recent angling survey noted that one out of four of the state's 600,000 licensed anglers participate in high Cascade lakes fishing opportunities and they are a dedicated group who say they return year after year. The project is funded through the sale of Oregon angling licenses and tags and the cost to benefit ratio of the project is significant.

Managers said that every dollar spent on the weeklong aerial trout stocking of Oregon's high lakes generates an additional 16 dollars to the Oregon economy by the anglers and campers who journey to the remote areas. Moberly, an

The air delivery trout project travels to more than 400 Oregon Cascade Range lakes in just one week.

avid fisherman and backpacker himself, added that the project provides unique Oregon angling opportunities to those willing to go the extra mile and find adventure: "It's rewarding to go into the wilderness with a rod and reel on your backpack so you can catch your dinner. If you've never been out to the wilderness to see some of these gorgeous lakes, you really owe it to yourself to get out there. Oregon is such a beautiful place."

Oregon Department of Fish and Wildlife, Salem Headquarters

Where: 4034 Fairview Industrial Drive SE, Salem, OR 97302

Web: Trout stocking schedules are available from www.dfw.or.us.

Phone: Fish Division: 503-947-6000

Watch the Episode: www.traveloregon.com/flyingtrout

15

The Kayak Shack

*W*hen it comes to summertime work, teens are lucky if they can find anything —washing cars, slinging burgers, or perhaps bagging groceries at the neighborhood store. So imagine the surprise that many visitors to the Oregon coast experience when they cross paths with a group of teens who have created a successful summer recreation business. It's called The Kayak Shack and is located on Alsea Bay at Waldport; it provides a pathway for youngsters who are eager to learn about business and help their community.

The beach may seem an unlikely place to find teens actually in school, but The Kayak Shack is unlike any class most high school students take because it's also a job that they create. "We really take it seriously; it's not a joke and we put in the hard labor like cleaning and caring for our kayaks and varied gear," said Amy Mullen. She is a 3-year veteran of The Kayak Shack team and added, "We also hire people based upon who's going to work the hardest and not who our friends are."

Six Waldport High School students work hard at The Kayak Shack motivated by this fact: it's in their best business interest to do so because it *is* their business.

The popular ecotourism kayaking company takes newcomers across the Alsea Bay Water Trail that also includes a delightful paddle into nearby

Students from Alsea High School own and operate The Kayak Shack.

Students like Maddie Parnell (left) are trained and certified to conduct tours across the Alsea Bay Canoe Trail.

"Lint Slough." The trips are led by certified guides and high school students like Maddie Parnell. She said it is "exciting to take people out on the water and teach them a recreation they've not tried before and show off the natural world and wildlife of Alsea Bay."

"The Kayak Shack started out as a business club with students pretty much running the operation," said Parnell. "We've learned so much from our teacher and business leader, Melissa Steinman. She guides us along as we put real-world experiences of operating a business into action." Steinman, a Waldport High School teacher, said the business grew out of course work. She said that each student who guides for The Kayak Shack is trained and certified through varied course work sponsored by the American Canoe Association: "I provide them with guidance and then say, 'Hey, where do we go from here and how do we make this better?'"

Steinman added that the Port of Alsea supports the student managed business with boats and a building, but the day-to-day operation including tours, boat maintenance, and even marketing is handled entirely by the teens. "These students brought with them that heart for caring about the local outdoors where they've grown up. I simply gave them the opportunity to become paddle professionals through certified course work. They each have a high level of care for their community and those two things go together to make a successful business."

There are more opportunities the students have explored, too, including spin-off ideas like T-shirts, sweatshirts, and caps that were designed by The Kayak Shack's marketing manager, Amy Mullen. She said that each purchase or guided trip not only helps their business, but also trickles through the greater Waldport economy too: "We make our clients tired and hungry and they will go out and eat at the nearby Salty Dawg Grill or other businesses close to us," said Mullen. "They may also spend the night in our local motels, so the money circulates locally and we're not the only beneficiaries."

On the bay, certified guide and high school senior Phil Hawkens said the nearly 2-mile round-trip into Lint Slough is best enjoyed on an incoming tide to help push the paddlers up the bay. He also noted that the skills he has developed at The Kayak Shack include basic boating, lifesaving, CPR, and leadership responsibilities that may help him find a career path in outdoor recreation: "This work has great responsibility as I'm a guide for up to four paddlers, so it's not kid stuff. I feel like an adult and must take care of my clients." The Kayak Shack team is "like family" and Hawkens hoped they would keep it that way in the future: a successful ecotourism business that helps the local community and a fine example of Oregonians helping each other.

Hawkens added that there's no finer landscape than Alsea Bay or a more scenic way to enjoy it than atop one of their kayaks: "Most people are surprised at how easy it is to paddle themselves across flat water—and how truly wonderful it is to be so close to the environment. I've seen eagles, osprey, deer, and elk and we always see something new on each trip." The ecotouring business is growing at a 30 percent annual rate each year as word of mouth about the student-guided tours spreads across Oregon. "These are the kids that I hope will live in my community, be my next-door neighbors, and run the businesses in my community," said Steinman. "The Kayak Shack helps them understand what it takes—the commitment and responsibility it takes to operate a business in their hometown—hopefully, it will pay off for each of them later in life too."

15 The Kayak Shack

Where: 365-B Port Street, Waldport, OR 97394

Web: www.whskayakshack.com

Phone: 541-563-4445

Watch the Episode: www.traveloregon.com/kayakshack

16

Upper Klamath Lake
Canoe Trail

*S*ummer mornings on Upper Klamath Lake arrive with dazzling sunshine and a cool, high-desert breeze. It's a place where wide, timeless vistas allow your imagination to wander among mountains, grassy meadows, broad lakes, ponds, and rich, mysterious marshlands. Listen closely for the music, what I like to call "Klamath Marsh music," a sometimes raucous and rowdy chorus of territorial birdsongs from winged species of all sorts twisting and turning and shaking their shadows across the grass and water. Ducks, geese, and shorebirds probe the muck of the marshes and can be seen defending their small nesting domains in the richness of vast Klamath Marsh National Wildlife Refuge. My first canoe trip into Klamath Marsh occurred by accident. Previously, I had been here solely to fish for the broad-shouldered, 4-pound Klamath rainbow trout famous in Northwest angling circles.

When the catching had been slow on one particular trip, a friend suggested something different. We traded in our outboard for paddles and his sleek aluminum fishing boat for a wooden canoe and found a new adventure at the north end of the marsh. The official Upper Klamath Canoe Trail begins near the Rocky Point Resort area and winds its way through shallows framed by cattails and lily pads. The trail is part of the larger system of national wildlife refuges and provides a unique view of huge numbers of birds that migrate here to breed and nest. The 15,000-acre marsh has been protected since 1928. The canoe trail was established in 1980. The marked 9.5-mile journey through the wetlands is divided into four segments: Recreation Creek, Crystal Creek, Wocus Cut, and Malone Springs. Each segment offers spectacular views of the marsh, mountains, and forest.

Recently, I enlisted the assistance of Darren and Jenifer Roe of ROE Outfitters to point out the special qualities of the canoe trail. Darren's first suggestion was to try to understand just why wetlands are so important: "The wetlands are certainly scenic—and everyone notices that right away, but the wetlands are also important because they clean the water. Much of this upper Klamath Lake is fed by springs that well up out of the ground, so it's reliably cold and that's good for the fish and the birds that travel here."

Klamath Marsh is unique in that some animal species or subspecies can be found here and nowhere else. Spring and summer ducks to watch for include blue-winged teal and cinnamon teal, northern shoveler, gadwall, American widgeon, and ruddy duck. In late summer watch for American white pelican, Caspian tern, and other shorebirds, including American bittern, Virginia rail, white-faced ibis, and sand-hill crane. You can also find colonies of yellow-headed and tricolored blackbirds.

As you slide through the marsh consider this fact: Up to 3 million ducks, geese, and other birds migrate annually through Klamath Marsh National Wildlife Refuge (part of a network of lands known as the Klamath Basin National Wildlife Refuge Complex) and over 260 species have been observed. The best time to paddle to observe the most bird activity is early morning or late evening. While birds are the most visible critters, many mammal species are at hand as well, so watch for beavers, muskrats, and river otters.

The trail segments can be accessed from either the Rocky Point or Malone Springs boat launches. The Rocky Point launch has a barrier-free toilet, boat dock, and fishing dock to serve people with disabilities. Please remain on the designated canoe trails to prevent disturbance to nesting species, and be sure to carry all your trash out with you. This is a day-use-only area and two canoeists can paddle about 2 miles an hour, so plan your trip accordingly. Canoes and skiffs can be rented at Rocky Point.

16A Rocky Point Resort

Where: 28121 Rocky Point Road, Klamath Falls, OR 97601
Web: www.rockypointoregon.com
Phone: 541-356-2287

16B ROE Outfitters FlyWay Shop

Where: 9349 US Highway 97 South, Klamath Falls, OR 97603
Web: www.roeoutfitters.com
Phone: 541-884-3825

Watch the Episode: www.traveloregon.com/klamathcanoe

Oregon's Invasive Species

*A*t Henry Hagg Lake in Washington County, state fishery biologist Rick Boatner spearheads a volunteer boat inspection station. He leads five teams of two inspectors each who will fan out across Oregon each year to inspect boats at varied locations. He reached into a small plastic container and pulled out a handful of small, drab-gray, quagga and zebra mussel shells. "This bunch came off one side of one prop at Lake Mead, Nevada . . . and as you can see, they cluster each other, so you get smaller ones on top of the bigger ones, so they grow on top of each other."

Boatner added that the invasive mussels have cost state governments in the Great Lakes area hundreds of millions of dollars over the past three decades. In that part of the country, the zebra mussel invasions have collapsed fisheries, taken over beaches, and clogged miles of pipelines. Each mussel filters a liter of water a day and removes nutrition from the water that in turn starves the fish that live in the area too. Boatner said, "It is the last thing we ever want to see happen in Oregon." They will be looking for signs of the mussels and snails that can hitchhike into Oregon's waterways on boats' motors, trailers—really, just about any marine surface. It's not just the boats, but the boots that anglers wear too—especially the anglers who fish in different rivers and lakes across the United States.

He said that the cure is easy enough: "Scrub. It's that simple. After you get out of the water and before you get to another water body. A small brush will take care of 90 percent of the problem right there." So how big is the risk of aquatic invasives coming to Oregon? Oregon State Marine Board aquatic invasives expert Glenn Dolphin said: "Oregonians should be very alarmed by the risk. It's serious because it will affect everything in our water-rich region." Dolphin said that the mussels threaten more than recreation because they can live on practically any surface, so they can easily infest drinking water pipelines, agriculture water lines, and hydroelectric production facilities too. "This is really the first program in Oregon that's been focused on the aquatic invasives. We are trying to get ahead of the curve and be proactive and preventative. This is really an aggressive first step that the state is taking on the aquatic invaders themselves."

The new aquatic invasive species (AIS) inspection program is paid through a 5 dollar permit for both motorized and nonmotorized boats alike. Motorized boat owners will see the increase in their boat registration. But if you paddle a canoe or a kayak or row down a white-water river in a watercraft that's 10 feet or longer, you'll need to buy the new Aquatic Invasive Species Prevention Permit for each boat that goes in the water. You must carry the AIS permit on your person when you are in the boat on an Oregon waterway. "We're asking people to look past the 5 dollar bill that you have to pay and look to where the money is going and what we're doing with that money," said Boatner. "This money doesn't get lost in the general fund; it's dedicated money that goes back into a direct benefit to the boaters that pay into it."

Recreation managers are posting new signs at many boat ramps across Oregon too. The posters ask boat owners to inspect their water-crafts and thoroughly drain and clean them. Meanwhile, Boatner noted that the battle lines are drawn—now is the time to make certain that the aquatic invasives don't land in Oregon waterways: "The simplest means and cheapest means is to deal with them right now, because once they become established, then we're going to deal with containment just to pro-tect what we take for granted today: fresh water and electricity at a cheap rate. Everything will change."

Oregon State Marine Board

Where: 435 Commercial Street NE, #400, Salem, OR 97309

Contacts: 503-378-8587; Fax: 503-378-4597

Watch the Episode: www.traveloregon.com/invasivespecies

August

17

East Lake Trout Are Back

The Oregon Department of Fish and Wildlife (ODFW) and local folks are restoring prized trout fishing at a premier Cascade Mountain lake: East Lake is an Oregon destination where unmatched Cascade Mountain scenery rules and warm hospitality is king. It's a timeless place perfect for building lasting family memories of camping time together in the great outdoors. East Lake has been renowned for its summer trout fishing for more than a century; anglers travel to the pristine lake that's set in the caldera of the Newberry National Volcanic Monument to fish for rainbow trout, brown trout, and kokanee. But in recent years, East Lake's famed trout fishing has been on the decline while the numbers of a nonnative fish species called tui (two-ee) chub have soared.

Early morning—when the air is cool and the light is soft, Central Oregon's East Lake is a marvel. It's the time of day when longtime angler Mike Cleavenger likes to catch the lake's famous kokanee and trout. He relies on lightweight rod, reel, and tackle, and a lure called Gibb's Minnow that he jigs just above the bottom in 35 feet of water. Cleavenger said the lure imitates an injured minnow: "I add three pieces of shoepeg corn onto the treble hook—two pieces are dyed red and the third is left natural . . . really adds to the effectiveness of the jig."

In minutes, my favorite fishing partner, Christine McOmie, hooked a gorgeous, deep-bodied 16-inch brown trout. Cleavenger said that the quality of the trout fishing had been on a steady decline since 2011. At one time, East Lake was one of the state's premier high Cascade Mountain lakes for catching rainbow trout, but it took a nosedive when the invasive tui chub took over the lake: "The chub were beating the kokanee and the trout to the insect food supply," noted the veteran angler. "The chub far outnumbered the trout and were more aggressive and faster at feeding. They simply exhausted the food supply."

Deep-bodied and dark-speckled brown trout are thriving once again in East Lake.

It's a similar story to the one that occurred at Southern Oregon's Diamond Lake back in 2006. The chub invasion was so bad that the prized rainbow trout didn't have a chance. In fact, most aquatic life in Diamond Lake had nearly died from the takeover by chub that had grown to number in the millions. "Back at that time," noted state fishery biologist Laura Jackson, "Diamond Lake had an estimated 98 million tui chub. About 90 million of them were juveniles that couldn't reproduce, but 8 million were reproductive so it really threw the lake's ecosystem out of balance." So, Diamond Lake was poisoned on purpose in 2006 with a common chemical pesticide called rotenone. Eleven boats spread hundreds of pounds of the chemical across each nook and cranny of the lake. Officials closed all access to the water for a time and the wait was worth it. "The treatment in 2006 was followed by trout stocking in 2007," added Jackson. "The little fingerlings that we released in June and July grew to be 8 inches and catchable by August or September. Now, it's once again a tremendous lake with a great trout fishery."

Four years ago, East Lake's fishermen and business owners worried the same chub takeover would happen at their prized lake. East Lake Resort co-owner Bruce Bronson said, "[The chub problem] was bad enough that individuals grouped together and called ODFW to ask: 'What can we do to bring back the trout to East Lake?'" ODFW determined that chemical treatment was not an option because—at nearly 300 feet deep—East Lake was too deep for effective treatment. So, the state partnered with local sportfishing groups and businesses to purchase special nets that were anchored around the lake's perimeter to intercept the chub. State fishery biologist Jennifer Luke managed the trapping operations and said the chub's biology worked well with their trapping plan: "Each July, the chub

More than 250,000 nonnative tui chub have been removed from East Lake the past 3 years.

swim into the lake's shallows at night to spawn. They hit our lead lines on these trap nets and follow each other into a holding area—once they get inside the net, they cannot swim out, so it works perfectly for catching chub."

Oregon State University Fishery Science students Jamie Bowles and Bonnie Schwartz are summer interns who assisted Luke with the trapping project. They checked five nets daily and removed the chub for disposal; the 3-year-old trapping effort has been remarkable. To date, they have removed a quarter million chub and in one day alone they caught more than 2,000 pounds of chub. "We get to see an interesting biological problem in real time," noted Bowles. "Plus, I love all the hard work and the fact that we are making a difference." Luke added that the project's success can also be measured by the abundance and quality of the trout and kokanee.

"The trout are healthier," said Luke. "They are not snaky and skinny but broad and fat, so we know we have reduced competition for the insect life in the lake. That's good news for fishermen. East Lake is back and these are the good old days."

17A East Lake Resort

Where: 22430 Paulina Lake Road, La Pine, OR 97739
Web: eastlakeresort.com
Phone: 541-536-2230
Watch the Episode: www.traveloregon.com/eastlaketrout

Inside the Newberry National Volcanic Monument

*W*hen the mood to move strikes my family, there's no better way to celebrate summer than our annual camping trip at the Newberry National Volcanic Monument near Bend. We leave busy US 97 behind and follow the lonesome trail high into the alpine reaches of the spectacular Newberry Caldera and my favorite high lakes called East and Paulina. Newberry National Volcanic Monument was established in 1990 and it includes over 50,000 acres of lakes, lava flows, and spectacular geologic features. The monument's summit is 7,985-foot Paulina Peak, which offers showcase views of the Oregon Cascades and the high desert. Retired geologist Bob Jensen noted, "On a clear day you can see from Washington's Mt. Adams to California's Mt. Shasta—and to the east you can see all the way to distant Steens Mountain."

Everywhere you look is a recreation heaven on earth offering snowcapped peaks, deep green forests, inviting pockets of ponds, and grassy meadows. Named for Dr. John S. Newberry, a scientist and early explorer with the Pacific Railroad Survey, the caldera (the center of the volcano) holds two lakes, Paulina Lake and East Lake. It's hard to believe as you drive through this mountainous area that you are within the caldera of a 500-square-mile volcano that remains very active seismically and geothermally. Geologists believe the park sits over a shallow magma body only 1.2 to 3.1 miles (2 to 5 kilometers) deep. At lower elevations like nearby Lava Butte you discover that the entire region's geologic history is a part of the remarkable Newberry National Volcanic Monument.

Jensen said you quickly learn that so much beauty was built upon devastating natural disasters that date back 75,000 years. "A key place to start is probably the Lava Lands Visitor Center to get a handle on the big story of what has happened in Central Oregon as recently as a thousand years ago. There is also the great viewpoint atop Lava Butte that overlooks the area. Then the Lava River Cave is nearby and easy to explore

Dress warm and don't forget a lantern and hiking boots to explore the underground world of Lava River Cave where it is a constant 42 degrees.

in summer. It's the longest lave tube in the state." If you go caving, be prepared with a lantern and dress for warmth—inside Lava River Cave it's a constant 42 degrees. Scott McBride, the national monument's manager, said that visitors to this national treasure can spend weeks exploring the monument's 50,000 acres and never see the same thing twice: "Visitors who take the time to turn off Highway 97 are completely surprised by what they almost missed and then completely excited that they didn't. It is the easy access to volcanic features, the types of recreation that you can do in the center of a caldera, which is essentially the heart of a massive volcano spreading out the size of Rhode Island."

The caldera also includes the Big Obsidian Flow, deposited 1,300 years ago by an eruption. This is one of the most intriguing parts of the crater—over a mile in length and 200 feet deep, with huge chunks of obsidian scattered about. The mile-long stroll puts you in the heart of gray pumice, brick-red lava, and ebony obsidian. Bart Wills, a geologist with the US Forest Service (USFS), said that Native Americans discovered the glasslike qualities of the obsidian and hand-tooled it into razor-sharp tools for hunting and cleaning game: "It's sharp like glass and it's very brittle; it holds a keen edge, but it breaks very easily. So once you've used obsidian as a tool—say, an arrow—the tip may break and they wouldn't be able to use it again. But, as you can see, there was no shortage of material."

Today the fractured, jagged ramparts of the volcano are topped by the pinnacle called Paulina Peak, but a glance down to East Lake's forested shore reminds me of my true interest in this site; camping has long been a tradition here. The first East Lake Resort was built in 1915, according to resort co-owner, Bruce Bronson. He told me with a chuckle, "A lot of people walk in the front door and ask, 'Where is the caldera? I came here to see the Newberry Caldera.' . . . Well, you're in it."

Bronson added that East Lake has long been a drawing card for the angling crowd; especially at daybreak, when trout and kokanee are on the bite: "Families have been coming here since the very beginning when it took much longer to get here, but then they stayed much longer too. Many come up with pictures of themselves in front of these same cabins when they were 5 or 6 years old and say, 'Boy, it hasn't changed much and it's like I remember.'" East Lake Resort's cabins offer all the comforts of home—just like the cozy café where no one ever walks away hungry. Rental boats put you on the water where fishermen troll or cast flies that entice big fish to bite. Nearby, two USFS campgrounds, called East Lake and Cinder Hill, offer more than 150 campsites for tent or trailer with plenty of lakeshore elbow room.

"People have a super outdoor experience in an atmosphere so clean and clear at 6,400 feet in elevation that the clouds seem but an arm's length away," added Bronson. That's certainly true and the stress melts away. There is no waterskiing or Jet Skiing on either Paulina or East Lakes, so life moves here at a slower pace.

"It's the camping, the hiking, fishing, and horseback riding," noted McBride. "Almost anything you can think of to do recreationally, we have it here in this national monument, and that is extraordinary."

17B Lava Lands Visitor Center
Where: 58201 South Highway 97, Bend, OR 97707
Phone: 541-593-2421

17C Cinder Hill Campground
Where: Forest Service Road 300, Deschutes National Forest, La Pine, OR 97739
Phone: 541-338-7869

Watch the Episode: www.traveloregon.com/newberrycrater

18

Luckiamute Landing
State Natural Area

*T*here are intriguing wildlife haunts that are as close as your own backyard and they are often hiding in plain sight—like the nearby Luckiamute River on the western fringe of the Willamette Valley in Polk County. It is home to mountain bike trails, wonderful waterfalls, and a new Oregon state park that was created for wildlife. The Little Luckiamute River cuts a beeline through eastern flanks of the Oregon Coast Range before it falls in an ear-shattering moment at Falls City, Oregon. The falls cascade through clefts in the exposed ancient basalt rock for nearly 40 feet, while less than 3 miles away another sort of "fall" happens when mountain bikers gather across a little piece of heaven called Black Rock Mountain.

The main attraction here is "free riding," where the riders catch big air across 500 acres of Oregon state forest. The volunteer organization that makes it all work is the Black Rock Mountain Bike Association, or BRMBA for short. Rich Bontrager, the association president, told me that the group is now 7 years old and 1,500 members strong. He noted that it all started with a simple dream: "I think we all need to help get people off the couch and out in the forest . . . to see that there's other stuff out here than the city pavement or a computer game. It's that sort of thing that draws folks—something new and different and exciting."

Luckiamute Falls drop some 40 feet through a deep cleft in the ancient basalt rock and provide a refreshing moment to rest.

The Little Luckiamute River is born in the Oregon Coast Range Mountains and flows more than 24 miles to join the Luckiamute River near Sarah Helmick State Recreation Site.

BRMBA member Todd Glasgow, a longtime rider, said that "feature" ideas are really born of the experiences that riders have as they take on trails across the United States. "Oh, yes—we ride other areas, see other things, and incorporate them into our own ideas and then take a spin on it. While some material is bought and some donated, a good majority of the wood that we use is fallen timber found in the forest." Whether jumping across 10-foot-high bike ramps or enjoying the freedom that comes from speeding down a forest trail on two wheels, the riders agree that there's something for every level of experience at Black Rock Mountain. "You're out here in the trees and you're away from everything else," noted Glasgow. "You're far away from the daily grind. You can have a stressful day or stressful week and you come out here and ride a bike—it's all gone."

Polk County offers more stress-free zones as the Luckiamute River flows into the Willamette Valley. In fact, when you pull in to Oregon's very first state park called Sarah Helmick State Recreation Site, located off US Highway 99, you will discover a hidden gem. "It's off the beaten path for sure, but the folks who've been coming here for decades like it that way," said Oregon State Parks Manager Bryan Nielsen. It's a treasure of a parkland that dates to 1922 when the Helmick family donated the land for future generations. "Back in the 1950s, camping really took off," said Nielsen. "Motor homes were invented, trailers were improving as technology was changing. The economy was improving and people had more free time. Parks like Sarah Helmick that really took off were valued for their peace and quiet." The park sprawls across 40 acres with plentiful picnic sites and play spaces under the shady limbs of giant oak and maple trees. "It's a great place to get out and stretch the legs," added Nielsen, "just to enjoy a beautiful park and get away from the stress of everyday life."

Less than 20 minutes east, the Luckiamute River slows and seems to meander on its way to meet the Willamette River as it courses through a state park where they're trying something new. Luckiamute Landing State Natural Area is parkland without rental cabins, trailer hookups, or play areas for the kids. It is a new park where they're turning the clock back to help restore wildlife habitat. Park ranger Steve DeGoey explained that the goal is to enhance nearly 1,000 acres for wildlife including varied bird life and even endangered western pond turtles.

Luckiamute is a day-use parkland that invites hikers or river paddlers; it is waiting for you to explore anytime. "We've planted about 440,000 shrubs and trees since 2011," added DeGoey. "Be sure to bring your binoculars when you come to visit. We've several miles of hiking trails. We have a variety of birds, and in spring, the wildflowers bloom too. Plus, two ponds that are home to western pond turtles that like to warm themselves on the logs. They can be a shy animal so be quiet and walk softly or they quickly jump into the water."

18A Luckiamute Landing State Natural Area

Where: Between US Highway 99W and I-5 N, about 5 miles northwest of Albany, OR

Web: www.oregonstateparks.org

Phone: 541-924-8492

18B Sarah Helmick State Recreation Site

Where: Off US Highway 99, 6 miles south of Monmouth, OR

Web: www.oregonstateparks.org

Phone: 541-924-8492 or 800-551-6949

Watch the Episode: www.traveloregon.com/luckiamuteriver

19

Wildflowers on an Iron Giant

*I*t is easy to escape the daily grind on a gas tank getaway to a wildflower bonanza along the trail to Oregon's "Iron Giant." On a dreamy summer morning, the South Santiam River flows fast and clear and provides a fine place to start a day that promises a simmering afternoon. US Forest Service Ranger Jennifer O'Leary said that Yukwah Campground puts you in touch with Cascade Mountain adventures: "There are so many recreation opportunities available along the river corridor; developed campgrounds and dispersed camping, river recreation, and lots of hiking trails."

The camping and especially the hiking are all right with me, 30 miles east of Sweet Home along US Highway 20, where the spacious, barrier-free Walton Ranch Interpretive Trail provides wheelchair accessibility and leads you up a gentle grade through a lichen-draped forest. The payoff for your hiking effort is a sprawling viewing platform that's more than a hundred feet long and gives you peekaboo views to the South Santiam River and a huge meadow beyond where Roosevelt elk are often seen. The short hike is a fine warm-up for a dandy just up the road. If time is on your side for a daylong excursion, discover the spectacular bursts and hues of an amazing array of red, blue, and yellow alpine wildflowers that

Through the aeons of time, oxidation has turned much of Iron Mountain a burnished red.

More than 300 wildflower species, including rock penstemon, can be found along the Iron Mountain Trail.

steal the scene at the little-known geologic wonder named Iron Mountain. This destination will challenge you with its 1.7-mile hike and 1,500 feet of elevation gain.

Cesar Barajas is an avid hiker who said that when he tackles Iron Mountain, he carries food, plenty of water and, of course, his camera. "The hike is not easy," noted Barajas. "You are definitely going to drop some sweat along the way, but the spectacular views and all the wildflowers make the trip so exciting." The Iron Mountain Trail leads through stands of Doug fir trees and up the side of the mountain at a moderate grade. It branches about halfway up—stay to the right and you'll soon be zigging and zagging along a series of switchbacks up an even steeper grade. There's quite an impressive show as you ramble through meadow after meadow exploding with wild color. Pause often, catch your breath, and savor the likes of sapphire lupine or crimson paintbrush—plus larkspur, penstemon, columbine, and scores of wildflower varieties always at your side. Practically every wildflower that grows in

The astounding panorama atop the Iron Mountain viewing deck is a welcome payoff for rest and relaxation.

long loop and it is on a unique geological formation of lava that bubbled up out of the earth aeons ago. It became a hard basalt feature that the Trask River could not cut through, so it went around and created the peninsula." Along the trail, watch for charred remains of burned-out old-growth trees from the four major fires, collectively called the Tillamook Burns, that roared through this country in the last century.

When you reach the river and the trail loop turns to take you back, you'll find picnic tables for a rivershore lunch—the perfect place to linger for a while. "It's a beautiful spot," said Seable, "especially when the river's down in summer! There's a nice beach for kids to play along the river and people can fish too." While salmon, steelhead, and cutthroat trout swim about, take some time to explore the river's nooks and crannies for something else—this is where the crawfish live.

I have been visiting the Trask River each summer for more than 40 years to explore the river's depths and catch small crustaceans called crawfish. My kids have grown up enjoying the area as well—sometimes with a mask and a snorkel to dive and catch the crawfish by hand—or with rod and reel and a chunk of bacon at the end of a line. You can also use a small wire-mesh trap (readily available at any sporting goods store) baited with a can of cat food.

Place the bait inside the trap as an attractant. The crawfish walk inside through the narrow funnel-like openings at either end. Once inside they can't seem to find the way back out. We attach a rope to the trap, toss it into a promising looking deep pool, and then tie off the rope to a tree. We may leave it in the river for a few hours, or if we're camping at the park, we leave it in overnight. We'll retrieve it the next morning and it's usually full of crawfish.

"You can find crawfish anywhere along the river in summer," noted state fishery biologist Robert Bradley. "Walk out into any of the pools and even swifter water and start flipping over rocks and you'll find some pretty quick. Folks can catch them by hand or with traps; it's a bit like crabbing in the bay only on a smaller scale. It's an abundant resource that people can enjoy all summer long."

No angling license or shellfish license is required to catch crawfish—and the limit is generous too: 100 crawdads per person per day is the daily limit. We tossed our trap into the drink and we spent the day lounging on the inviting beach. When the mood to move, or the heat of the sun, struck us—we would scamper into the river.

My youngsters and I have always had a ball along the Trask River—diving, exploring, searching the river bottom's nooks and crannies, and rolling over submerged rocks to see what secrets the river held. Whenever a sizable crawfish (we'd made a vow not to keep any under 5 inches in length) appeared, the youngsters would carefully maneuver hands to capture the critter by its head, just behind its two impressively large pincer claws. Catching crawdads by hand is fun sport and a delightful way to beat the summer heat.

Crawfish or crawdads or just plain "dads" are a creepy crawly kind of critter that kids love to catch and they taste good too. We often prepare our catch using my good friend's recipe (see below for Birt Hansen's Basic Crawfish Boil). The taste of fresh-cooked crawfish is sublime—a very mild shrimplike taste that's somewhat delicate. The taste, the setting, and the adventure offer a stark contrast to the broiling sun during the heat of summer—a perfect cap to a day's adventure that your family will want to try soon. Crawfishing and summertime confirm what you may suspect: you're never too old to be a kid again—especially during the dog days of summer.

Birt Hansen's Basic Crawfish Boil

This recipe relies on a handful of simple ingredients.

2 quarts water	½ cup pickling spice
1 cup vinegar	4 bay leaves
½ cup salt	2 to 3 pounds crawfish

Bring the water, vinegar, and seasonings to a boil, then add the crawfish. Cook no longer than 3 to 4 minutes. Overcooked, the crawfish become rubberlike and flavorless.

Spread out a sheet or two of newspaper on a picnic table, dump out the steaming crawdads, and dig in. Grab the tail section, pull it away, and simply peel off the tail shell—everything else will pull right out. Same with the claws—crack them open and pick out the meat.

This is hands-on eating at its finger-licking finest—and that's best with youngsters who really get into their meals. This recipe easily serves a group of 4 and is best enjoyed with a twist of lemon over the small pile of cooked crawdads!

---

20 Trask County Park

Where: 25455 Trask River Road, Tillamook, OR 97141

Web: www.rockawaybeach.net

Phone: 503-842-4559

Watch the Episode: www.traveloregon.com/oregoncrawfish

September

21

Songbird Science

*S*eptember is a season of change in the great Oregon outdoors and it can be the best time to see the natural world at work, especially if you find a front row seat to an age-old wildlife story at Snag Boat Bend. It is a public place where "songbird science" takes flight each morning when bird migration kicks into high gear. Certainly, there are many well-known waterfowl and raptor species that make journeys that reach thousands of miles from sub-Arctic areas to Central and South America. But other wildlife migrations are harder to spot, like the scores of songbird species that take flight each September and October for warmer climes. As an annex to the more popular William L. Finley National Wildlife Refuge, Snag Boat Bend Unit is quiet most times of the year. But that's changed each September when a team of scientists and biologists conduct songbird surveys to learn more about many bird species that we rarely see.

"We call it the 'dawn chorus' when the birds become very active as the sun rises," said Oregon State University (OSU) Assistant Professor Dana Sanchez. She leads a team of OSU researchers in a partnership with US Fish and Wildlife biologists to capture and band as many songbirds on the refuge as possible from August into early October. Sanchez added, "We are right in the middle of fall migration and here at Snag Boat Bend we are able to detect them and get them in hand."

They "get them in hand" with special nets, explained federal biologist Molly Monroe: "It's called a mist net and once it is set up you will understand why it's called that." Mist nets reach 8 feet high and they can be as long as 60 feet. They are set up the way you might set up a badminton net in the backyard, except that the nylon mesh of a mist net is so fine that the net is nearly invisible. "It's pretty hard for the birds to see," added Monroe. "They will hit the net and then they will

Visitors to Snag Boat Bend can lend a hand and release the banded songbirds.

fall into these pockets of net that are folded into the mesh. It's effective and usually doesn't take us long to catch songbirds that are moving in the early morning light."

She was right. Following a short wait, the team inspected six mist nets that had been set up on the refuge property that is adjacent to the Willamette River. The nets captured a remarkable array of birds and included three spotted towhees, a Swainson's thrush, a common yellowthroat, and a song sparrow. Each tiny bird was slowly and patiently untangled from the nets by team members and then delivered to a banding station where "care and caution" were the bywords for the folks handling the fragile songbirds. Each bird was weighed, measured, and examined before a numbered aluminum band was placed on one of its legs. The numbered band helps the research team learn more should any of the birds be recaptured along a migration route that can reach to South America.

It is remarkable work that offers many fascinating insights to the world of small songbirds. For example, during fall migration, Monroe said that the songbirds mostly travel at night and then rest and forage for food during the day. And the songbird journeys are nothing short of amazing for birds so tiny they weigh ounces, not pounds. "Some species migrate from as far away as Alaska all the way to South America—and then return to their northern nesting grounds in spring," noted Monroe.

Snag Boat Bend was selected for the survey because it offers more than 300 acres of intact riparian habitat along the Willamette River. Sanchez offered that there is concern for songbird populations because their preferred habitat is increasingly rare: "It used to be far more common in the Willamette Valley, but with development this riparian habitat of cottonwoods, willows, and ash has become something of a rarity. We suspect these are valuable patches for breeding as well as for migrating birds. Our work will help confirm whether that is true or not."

Snag Boat Bend Wildlife Refuge is a good place for you to migrate to as well according to Monroe: "There is a hiking trail from the parking area that goes out to a viewing blind. When the water is high you can see a lot of waterfowl and in the summer the area has a good population of western pond turtles that bask themselves in the warm sun atop floating logs." Refuge visitors can watch the project too—maybe even lend a hand with a bird release. It's also a good chance to learn more about the little known songbirds of the Oregon outdoors.

21A Snag Boat Bend Unit

Where: Located 1 mile east of Corvallis (cross the Willamette River bridge), then south 11 miles on Peoria Road. Watch for signs. The boardwalk at the trailhead parking area leads to the wildlife blind.

Phone: William L. Finley National Wildlife Refuge: 541-757-7236

Watch the Episode: www.traveloregon.com/songbirdscience

The Positive for Peregrines

*I*t's a moment that takes your breath away as two peregrine falcons tangle in midair above downtown Portland. According to Portland Audubon Society Conservation Director Bob Sallinger, it's an uncommon sight that's more common than you'd think: "These birds can dive at 200 miles an hour and take other birds on the wing. They're just a truly spectacular bird." The air battle was the result of a female falcon protecting her nest from an interloper—the nest is located on the underside of the Fremont Bridge. Sallinger noted that it's a great sign to see peregrines in Portland: "We didn't have any peregrines and now we have peregrines chasing other peregrines out of the area, so things are going in the right direction."

That wasn't always true. Decades ago, peregrines were in big trouble because the chemical pesticide DDT was linked to a nosedive in peregrine production. When the chemical was banned in the 1970s the birds recovered. Sallinger noted that the Fremont Bridge peregrines began nesting there in 1994 and they have raised dozens of offspring ever since. They have thrived there because the habitat is perfect. "A bridge like the Fremont looks to a peregrine like a cliff; it has ledges like a cliff and to a large degree, it functions like a cliff. It is the most successful nesting site in the state of Oregon, right here in the middle of downtown Portland. We can be proud of that." The peregrine's comeback from the brink of extinction has been remarkable: in 1970 there were zero nesting birds in Oregon; today there are more than 100 nesting pairs. So, the state fish and wildlife agency delisted, or removed, them from the state's endangered species list in 2007.

The birds have thrived not just downtown but across Oregon. For example, over the years Cape Meares National Wildlife Refuge in Tillamook County has been the scene for peregrine nesting on a cliff 600 feet above the ocean surf. A number of years ago I visited with Bus

Engsberg who enjoyed a front row perch to watch the activity. He had shot video over several years that showed two peregrines that raised dozens of young each year for more than a decade. "I've talked to ornithologists across the country; people studying them in the Rocky Mountains and the Grand Canyon, and as soon as they see this site they say, 'My gosh, Bus, you've got it made.' It's the best place you can imagine." Sallinger agreed and added that when given a chance, peregrine falcons adapt to every environment in the state. "When people think about an urban environment they don't typically think about wildlife, but this is really a testament that what we do in our urban ecosystems makes a difference." A positive difference that will keep peregrines soaring across the Oregon skyline.

21B Cape Meares National Wildlife Refuge

Where: About 10 miles west of Tillamook on the
Three Capes Scenic Route

Web: www.fws.gov/oregoncoast/capemeares

Phone: 541-867-4550

22

Siltcoos River
Canoe Trail

*T*here is something special about seeing the great outdoors from a coastal river's point of view; the paddling experience is filled with wonder and surprise as you paddle from freshwater toward the ocean—especially along the Siltcoos River Canoe Trail in the heart of the Oregon Dunes. I recently joined Coos Bay paddler and ecotourism teacher Marty Giles, whose Wavecrest Discoveries ecotour company can take you to places that fill you with wonder and surprise for all the wildlife you encounter along the waterway.

Giles noted that the Siltcoos River is characterized by little current, no rapids, and the splendor of nature always by your side on the 3.5-mile-long protected water trail. She said there is a tremendous amount of sensory experiences packed into a half-day trip. "It flows through the heart of the Oregon Dunes National Recreation Area," said Giles. "People come from all over to experience 32,000 acres of sand, forest, rivers, and lakes amid the only temperate sand dunes in North America."

The Dunes National Recreation Area stretches more than 42 miles from Florence to Coos Bay and it is an Oregon landmark for outdoor recreation. You may well wonder just where all the sand came from too. "It came from the mountains," said US Forest Service (USFS) spokesperson Gayle Gill. "It all started in mountains of the Cascade Range thousands of years ago when glaciers melted and carried debris—sandy sediments—to the ocean and deposited

Shorebirds are easy to spy from the cozy confines of a sea kayak on the Siltcoos River Canoe Trail.

The Siltcoos River Canoe Trail allows visitors to travel from the freshwater to the ocean.

them out there. There are no rocky headlands here to prevent the sand from going to the ocean and the waves and wind then pushed it all back up on the land and that's what we have today in the Oregon Dunes."

Our starting point was the USFS Lodgepole Picnic Area; a day site along the Siltcoos River and just a stone's throw from Jessie M. Honeyman Memorial State Park, but the Siltcoos River felt a million miles away from human hubbub and noise. The river zigs and zags sharply at low tide and many of the river bends are framed by huge sandbanks. At ebb tide, we watched for logs and branches that were silent and sobering reminders that we had to negotiate an adventurous trail. "It courses from a narrow freshwater stream environment out to the estuary and close to ocean," said Giles. "The character of the river changes quite a bit and like most coastal streams there will be a lot of branches and logs and woody debris in the stream."

Cyndy Williams and her husband, JC Campos, had never done anything like this trip before, but they loved each minute of it. The couple traveled from their home in Portland for the daylong adventure. As the pair paddled, they soon discovered that the Siltcoos River offered intimate moments where they felt close to nature: "Ohhh, I am hooked," noted JC with a smile. "Kayaking is now one of our new choices to get around Oregon." Before long, our downriver journey slowed across the much wider waterway on approach to the sea. Tall sedge grasses seemed to wave us along from shore. We also noticed important warning signs along the estuary shore—plus roped-off areas that marked a beach closure in effect from March 15 to September 15. This area of the Siltcoos River and Estuary is important because it protects nesting sites for small shorebirds called snowy plovers, a federally protected and endangered species.

We were soon 3 miles from the start and in the heart of the estuary—it was a view that offered sneak peeks across the sand of the crashing ocean surf. We also noted varied shorebird species that were probing the muck of the marshes; often they were right by our sides. It is the sort of adventure that will set your clock back—guaranteed! The Siltcoos River Canoe Trail is open anytime. No permits are required to paddle the Siltcoos River Trail but a US Forest Service Northwest Forest Pass (available for day or annual purchase) is required at the Lodgepole Picnic Area. Central Coast Watersports in Florence provided our boats, paddles, and PFDs; they even delivered to our launch site at the Lodgepole Picnic Area and picked them up at the end of our trip.

22A Siltcoos River Canoe Trail
Where: About 6 miles south of Florence in the Oregon Dunes National
Recreation Area
Phone: 541-271-3611

22B Wavecrest Discoveries
Where: 852 South 12th Street, Coos Bay, OR 97420
Phone: 541-267-4027

22C Central Coast Watersports
Where: 1901 US Highway 101, Florence, OR 97439
Phone: 541-997-1812 or 800-789-3483

Watch the Episode: www.traveloregon.com/siltcooscanoe

23

In the Heart of
the Gorge

*T*here are so many faces to the Columbia River Gorge: a place where light and shadow dance across ancient basalt cliffs that rise hundreds of feet above a river that takes the breath away for its size and power. It is a place where you can discover vivid scenery that fills the senses as you trek across hiking trails that lead you into new territory. Perhaps your journey allows you to go face to face with the most amazing collection of thundering waterfalls in Oregon. There is so much, so close, and so easy to reach when you visit the heart of the gorge at Cascade Locks.

"Cascade Locks is indeed the heart of the gorge," noted Cascade Locks resident Holly Howell. "Our community is surrounded by the Columbia River Gorge National Scenic Area and that is why our hillside views are so pristine." Howell is also the development manager for the Port of Cascade Locks and she said it isn't a matter of finding enough to do in the gorge, but rather "finding enough time to do it all."

We visited the newest public venue for hikers and bikers called the EasyCLIMB (Cascade Locks International Mountain Biking) Trail on the eastern edge of town. The new 3-mile-loop trail is awash in color with brilliant blue camas and chocolate lilies, plus an unmatched view to the Columbia River. We also enjoyed a view of a nesting pair of osprey that was raising their young. Howell added, "The trail was built by volunteers who gave more than 1,200 hours of labor to design and build a family friendly trail to draw people to the sport of mountain biking but it has been embraced by a lot of our locals who enjoy walking their dogs too."

The Cascade Locks Marine Park is a spacious public setting for a picnic lunch and also the launching point for 2-hour river trips aboard the *Columbia*

Gorge Sternwheeler. The park also offers visitors a chance to learn more about the "real" Cascade Locks in the local Historical Museum. Pat Power is the volunteer caretaker of the small museum that offers a stunning photo collection chronicling the building of the locks. "Before the locks were built," noted Power, "boats from Portland could only come up the Columbia River to an area near the Bonneville Dam—there they would dock and everything was off-loaded and transported up here to bypass the dangerous Cascade Rapids. From here, they could get onto another sternwheeler and continue further east." The photo collection captures one of Oregon's most ambitious construction projects of the 1800s that included over 3,000 feet of canal, with three giant steel gates, and which took more than 20 years to complete.

When it opened in 1896, it offered easy passage for steamboats delivering food, supplies, and people up and down the river. The Cascade Locks Historical Museum was part of the project too. It was built by the Army Corps of Engineers in 1905. Power explained, "They built three houses here and they still stand. Each house was aligned with the gates in the lock. The lock masters and their families lived in the homes and they went right out the front door to work each day—just a few yards away."

Back in the park, you'll also notice one of the newest features of the community—an art in the park project that includes three bronze statues by a local bronze sculptor, Heather Söderberg-Greene. The statues include Sacajawea and the great Newfoundland dog named Seaman. Both were members of the famed Lewis and Clark expedition that passed this way more than two centuries ago. Cascade Locks is the sort of timeless place that invites you to sit, put your feet up, and watch the river and the world flow by—and it's waiting for you—anytime.

23A Port of Cascade Locks

Where: 355 Wa Na Pa Street, Cascade Locks, OR 97014

Web: portofcascadelocks.org

Phone: 541-374-8619

Watch the Episode: www.traveloregon.com/cascadelocks

Dinosaurs with Fins?

O h, come on, Dad, there's no such thing as a dinosaur these days. I know all about dinosaurs and they died out 60 million years ago. I learned that in class." Many years ago, my 10-year-old son had insisted on this point for more than an hour as we cruised east of Portland on Interstate 84 toward Bonneville Dam. Eric was strongly convinced that there couldn't possibly be ("no way, no how") any living prehistoric animal species in our corner of the world. His determination was engraved upon an ever-deepening furrowed brow, so this was going to be a very tough sell for me. "Well, son," I slowly, politely, offered, "the fact is there is an ancient critter living here in the Northwest that is pretty well-known in some circles. It's a species whose history reaches back 200 million years. That's way before T-Rex's time, huh?"

"No way, no way, no way," he chimed. "There are no more dinosaurs!"

Eric was stumped for a research topic for a science class assignment, and I had an idea that might help him and perhaps surprise and teach many of his fellow students too. As we pulled into the parking area of the Bonneville Fish Hatchery, adjacent to the sprawling, monumental complex at Bonneville Dam, I had a plan to teach the youngster that there really was a dinosaur of a species alive and well in Oregon.

I love to visit the largest and most tourist-friendly fish hatcheries in Oregon each summer. We strolled past several gorgeous and glorious flower beds decked out with spectacular roses, marigolds, and impatiens whose blossoms were peaking like some colorful parade. "Well," I hinted, "this animal swims," hoping my clues might pique his youthful curiosity. "And it lives in rivers, but it also migrates to the ocean. It doesn't have scales, but it does have fins, and it can grow to a gigantic size, say 10 or 11 feet long. Any ideas?"

"Oh, Dad, I can't think of any." He was puzzled. I smiled, and together we ambled to the newest feature of the 6-acre facility: the home of "Herman the Sturgeon."

"A sturgeon!" he exclaimed. "Wow!"

Two 1-inch-thick Plexiglas windows are all that separate 450-pound Herman the Sturgeon from his adoring fans at Bonneville Hatchery in the Columbia Gorge. Herman is a 9-foot-10-inch-long white sturgeon, probably 70 years old, and a member of a fish family dating back some 200 million years. The Oregon Department of Fish and Wildlife (ODFW), working closely with the Oregon Wildlife Heritage Foundation, had designed the home for Herman to give him room to move about in a natural setting while allowing visitors to stay dry while watching him below water level.

The pond measures 30 feet by 100 feet and is about 10 feet deep, and unless you're a Columbia River fisherman, you've never been able to see a sturgeon so well, or to learn about their biology from well-designed information panels located near the windows. For the most part, these giants of the Northwest are bottom dwellers, and their pea-sized eyes don't allow them to see much in the murky depths of a river, so they rely upon four hairlike projections called barbels that are located at the ends of their snouts. These help the fish find food and feel their way along the river bottom. Instead of scales, sturgeon have tough skin and rows of bony, diamond-shaped plates along their lateral sides and down their top sides, or dorsals. The plates are called scutes (pronounced skoots), and biologists think of them as a sort of fish armor. It seems that in prehistoric times, sturgeon were entirely covered by these scutes for protection against even larger predator fish. Sturgeons also have upturned, sharklike tails and skeletons largely made of cartilage and less of bone. Sturgeon historically migrated throughout the Columbia River basin to the Pacific Ocean and can grow to 20 feet, weigh a thousand pounds or more, and live for more than a hundred years.

The first reference to a sturgeon named "Herman" occurred in 1925 at either the Bonneville or the Roaring River Hatchery near Scio. The very first report of a sturgeon named "Herman" occurred in 1935 when a former game commissioner raised the fish to be shown each year at the Oregon State Fair. This Herman was stolen from the Roaring River Hatchery in the middle of the night. Other "Hermans" have fulfilled the role since then.

The current facility features interpretive signs and displays and is open to the public throughout the year. The department also makes it available to school groups as an educational destination. As we gazed through the windows, Eric was not only impressed by Herman's length and girth, but also by the fact that even larger Hermans are alive and well in the Columbia. "Wow! That's pretty cool, Dad!" Eric snapped photos of

At Bonneville Fish Hatchery, you can go eyeball to eyeball with 10-foot-long "Herman the Sturgeon."

Herman and then scrambled for another view. "A living dinosaur. I've got something really special to write about for my science project now."

Herman is not the only attraction at the hatchery. A nearby viewing room allows visitors each fall to watch hatchery staff spawn chinook and coho salmon, and visitors can walk along the dozens of raceways where the department rears millions of tiny salmon and steelhead for release each spring. For a quarter, visitors can feed brood trout and other fish. Bonneville is one of thirty-six operating fish hatcheries in Oregon, many of which also offer fish and wildlife viewing opportunities.

Greg Davis, ODFW's Bonneville Hatchery manager, recently told me, "You are literally face to face with really big sturgeon; as close as 6 inches away, separated only by a thick piece of glass. We consider it our little aquarium." At the Bonneville Fish Hatchery's Sturgeon Exhibit, you will slow down to enjoy the show. A show of fish that is. Davis noted, "There isn't another opportunity that I know of in Oregon where you can view a sturgeon quite like this—underwater—it's a unique opportunity to see a large 10- or 12-foot-long sturgeon up close and personal."

Bonneville Hatchery has long been a unique destination for good reason. Over a century ago, the state facility raised thousands of baby fish for release. Back then, a long time before roads, the railroad was the only way to transport baby fish and then transfer them to the horse and pack trains that would trek into distant Oregon lakes and streams. These days, Bonneville Hatchery raises 11 million salmon, steelhead, and trout across a facility that's a most amazing parklike setting. "It's a great tribute to our ground staff," said Davis. "The grounds are beautiful—flowers and gorgeous plants throughout and it's a fine place to spend a Saturday afternoon close to Portland. Best of all, it is also free."

Since 1998, the Sturgeon Exhibit has given up to half a million visitors a year the chance to see a species seldom seen so close. "We hear ooohs and ahhhs all of the time from the visitors," added Davis. "Folks are so impressed to walk up and see something that huge that is slowly swimming past them, almost seeming to eye the visitors as they pass by." But let Bonneville Fish Hatchery be just the start of your journey to other gigantic discoveries in the Columbia River Gorge.

As you travel east on I-84, make time to stop, learn, and experience rich lessons in natural and cultural history at the Columbia Gorge Discovery Center and Museum in The Dalles. Since 1997, the Discovery Center has been the showcase setting and interpretive site for the National Scenic Area in the Columbia River Gorge. The Discovery Center's awesome entrance will captivate and leave you spellbound. Spokesperson Roxie Pennington said, "We're perched on one of the most phenomenally beautiful scenic outlooks in the gorge. As you walk inside our entrance and gaze up and through the pillars, you are drawn out of the glass wall to see the distant Klickitat Hills and more sky than most people see in a day." Spokesperson John Connolly added, "The Discovery Center is far more than dramatic scenery. The center links people to Oregon's rich cultural histories too—framed by the beauty and immensity of it all. It's a beautiful area to come celebrate and it's right out our backdoor."

23B Bonneville Hatchery

Where: 70543 NE Herman Loop, Cascade Locks, OR 97014
Web: www.dfw.state.or.us
Phone: 541-374-8393

23C Columbia Gorge Discovery Center and Wasco County Museum

Where: 5000 Discovery Drive, The Dalles, OR 97058
Web: www.gorgediscovery.org
Phone: 541-296-8600

Watch the Episode: www.traveloregon.com/dinosaurswithfins

24

Lewis and Clark
Paddled Here

O n a clear day, the view atop Bradley State Scenic Viewpoint to the Columbia River is breathtaking. Picnic tables invite you for a longer stay at this prime day-use site just off US Highway 30 near Astoria, where the birds-eye view to the river invites a closer shoreline inspection. So, not long ago I joined a group of paddlers who gathered to explore the Lower Columbia River's backwater sloughs and islands not far from the Bradley Viewpoint. Steve Gibons is owner and lead guide of Scappoose Bay Kayaking and he said that the Lower Columbia River's nooks and crannies provide paddlers a wealth of waterways. "At this time of year, you cannot ask for better weather—cooler and milder—so we're going to paddle upstream (from the Knappa Docks) and then cut into a special site in a Sitka spruce forest that has stood for centuries and there are two easy-to-reach sloughs that will put us right in the thick of things."

Blind Slough Swamp is certainly the thick of things; it is a Nature Conservancy Preserve of over 800 acres of soggy swampland with no land access. Blind Slough is the last sizable intact Sitka spruce and tidal-influenced swamp forest of the Columbia River, a habitat type that once stretched from Tillamook Bay north to southeast Alaska. It is home to salmon, beaver, river otter, bald eagles, and several other wildlife species. Fortunately, it has been protected by The Nature Conservancy since 1992. The swamp is a braid of channels, separated by acre-sized (or larger) islands. The slough is reminiscent of some distant southern bayou, but of dense willow, alder, and immense Sitka spruce. Some trees rise

Lightweight kayaks have an easy entry at the Knappa Docks.

You'll enjoy the million dollar view to the Columbia River from Bradley State Scenic Park.

200 feet or more and are 400 or more years old. The native vegetation is a jungle so thick you cannot walk into the islands, but when paddling through the backwater sloughs inside a stable kayak, the travel is easy and pleasant.

In this part of the Columbia River dotted by scores of islands that are separated by dozens of sloughs, a boat is the only way to get around. Gibons insisted that safety starts with a life jacket: "It is a state law that you must have one in the boat, but it's our rule that says you wear it at all times." The huge swamp forest dates to the 1600s, and Gibons called the trees, "absolute giants." "It was the predominant tree of the coastal northwest 200 years ago," noted Gibons. "The Sitka stands ran all the way up the western coastline to Alaska. Some of the trees reach 4 feet in diameter so to have a preserve like this is very special."

Historically, these areas flooded each spring from Columbia River runoff, so over time the silt built up and the islands grew larger. The big old Sitka trees could take root and adapt to the moist soil. Along the southern edge of the Columbia River, water is washing through the preserve all of the time and that makes it a rich place for salmon, waterfowl, and the larger predators like osprey, bald eagles, and even bears.

Keep this in mind too: although only a short 80 miles from Portland, you are in the middle of nowhere. There are very few places in western Oregon that allow that sense of escape and that is not lost on the other paddlers who joined our group on a fine September morning. "I've never seen anything like this anywhere else," said longtime paddler Bonnie Gibons. "It's the size of the trees, the quiet; just being able to experience the outdoors here is wonderful."

When I visit Blind Slough I often wonder whether Lewis and Clark's Corps of Discovery would even recognize it, considering the incredible changes time has brought to the Lower Columbia River. The enormous waterway bears little resemblance to the region traveled by the explorers of 1805. And when pioneers arrived 40 years later, mining, timber harvest, and fisheries soon followed. In the early twentieth century, the massive Grand Coulee and Bonneville hydroelectric projects began to tame the river's wildness. In little more than a century, human economic activity and development forever changed the river's free-flowing character. One net result is that much of the river's natural history has been lost, or at best is very difficult to find.

One thing is certain: The wildlife ties you to the landscape in a way that builds appreciation and understanding, and in a way, nature's touch at Blind Slough helps restore your soul. "I find it rejuvenating," added Tracey Cole. "I just feel younger getting out on the water and this is not very far from home." Of all the different ways I've journeyed throughout Oregon, paddling is the most intimate way to touch nature. It's easy and quiet, and you never know what you're going to see: perhaps an eagle roosting in a towering spruce, or a beaver or muskrat cruising by, maybe even a pond turtle basking on a log in the warm, waning afternoon sun. Paddling offers time well spent in the Oregon outdoors.

Note: Blind Slough is accessible only by canoe or small boat. The tides here can be strong and so can the winds. Please respect private-property signs and avoid the log rafts. May, June, and September are excellent times to visit the Blind Slough Preserve.

24A Blind Slough Swamp

Where: Lower Columbia River (approximately River Mile 27), east of Astoria, OR
Web: www.nature.org
Phone: 503-802-8100

24B Old Scappoose Bay Kayaking

Where: 57420 Old Portland Road, Warren, OR 97053
Web: www.scappoosebaykayaking.com
Phone: 503-397-2161

Watch the Episode: www.traveloregon.com/blindslough

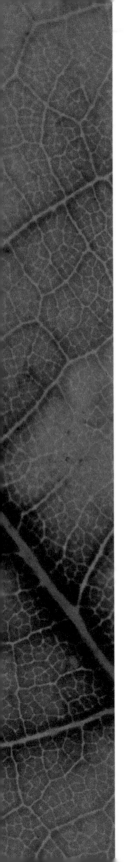

Fall

Grant McOmie's Outdoor Talk— Bullets and Greed

*W*ildlife stories are a challenge for all of the right reasons Many species are elusive, even secretive because they have adapted perfectly to their habitats. So, no surprise that the wildlife story genre is a test of a reporter's patience, especially when I am eager to observe and report on wildlife behavior. The experiences of reporting on wildlife have allowed me to work with the unsung heroes of the Fish and Wildlife Division of the Oregon State Police (OSP). They are an elite corps of men and women who work long hours in lonely outposts and their jobs are 24-7. There is no rest for Oregon's game cops. I began covering Fish and Wildlife enforcement's

efforts to protect and preserve fish and wildlife species in 1983. In those early years, I was intrigued by the effectiveness and the simplicity of the techniques that were used to catch outdoor outlaws who practiced "bullets and greed" across the vast stretches of Oregon. I have reported on scores of arrests made by game wardens who told me that large and well-organized poaching rings were illegally killing more deer, elk, bear, and other species. Poaching is a tough crime to solve because the handful of state police game officers cannot be everywhere at all times to enforce fish and game laws.

One of the most effective tools utilized by game officers is a fake critter named Scruffy! It is a full-sized, stuffed deer that comes with or without antlers. Some of the Scruffy decoys even move; the heads can turn from side to side and the tails wag back and forth. The movements are controlled via a handheld remote that reaches from as much as a hundred yards away. In enforcement circles, Scruffy is known by a more formal name: the W-E-D, or Wildlife Enforcement Decoy. But out in the field, most officers I have worked with across Oregon call it *Scruffy*. No matter what it's called, I have seen it effectively catch folks who hunt at night, without licenses, or shoot at Scruffy from inside their vehicles; all are clear violations of the hunting regulations and the spirit of the hunting ethic called "fair chase." I've also heard Scruffy called many other things by people who were caught in the act of violating game laws, including the "Dummy Deer," "Ol' Fake Out," "Dead Eye," plus many expletives too mean, too nasty, and certainly undeserved.

Suffice to say, those who are caught illegally shooting at Scruffy remember the moment forever, not only from the citation, but often times by their appearance in one of our news stories. It has been remarkable how a simple stuffed deer catches outlaws in the act of committing crimes against nature.

The success of Scruffy was so great that it wasn't long into the '90s when full-sized elk decoys followed and are now widely used during elk hunting seasons too. Recently, OSP Sergeant Todd Hoodenpyl told me that the agency's fake elk herd continues to serve the purpose of catching people in the act of violating Oregon's game laws. "Our officers seem to respond to more and more elk complaints from the legal hunters each year," said Hoodenpyl. "Dead elk are found dead on the ground out of season by our officers, or hunters will find illegal elk that are killed and left to rot. So, the fake elk are tools that provide one way we can catch the violators. It doesn't get any better."

Usually, the full-sized replicas are placed within easy sight along a well-traveled road during fall hunting season. Most of the elk decoys show signs of use—not on the front side, but on the backside where multiple holes mark the bullet exits and show how well the decoys have been used during the season. Officers have told me that they know the elk decoys will be shot at—they just wish more of the shooters were legal hunters. "Many hunters stop and look at the fake elk and then move on," noted Hoodenpyl. "We'd like to see that happen every time, every day." But it doesn't. Despite the fact that the fake elk don't move, some people pull up to the decoys, take aim, and fire several times. Officer John King said that during a recent hunting season, as many as 80 percent of the people who stopped and shot at the fake elk didn't have the proper licenses or tags.

I recently joined a decoy operation in Tillamook County and watched a truck slowly pull into a scene where two fake cow elk were set in a clearing, less than a hundred yards away. The driver stepped out of his truck—took aim and fired three times. Then his passenger got out, moved to the front of the vehicle, and took aim on the still standing cow elk and shot too. The officers quickly arrived on the scene, asked each man for their licenses and tags, and then explained to the passenger that he violated Oregon game law by not having the proper tag. To the officer's surprise, the man denied that he even shot at the cow elk. When the officer explained that a news crew had videotaped the entire scene, the man continued to deny that he took a shot and then asked to see the video. And so I showed him. Suddenly, the scofflaw admitted what he'd done and he received a citation.

"The violators are greedy," said Sergeant Hoodenpyl. "The decoys are targets and the shooters may or may not have a tag or hunting license, but too many have the attitude that they are going to put an elk down on the ground and figure out the tags later. It just reduces the amount of elk that legal hunters are able to harvest." The fake deer and elk are effective tools that catch people who would steal Oregon's wildlife resources from legal hunters and from the public.

Wildlife enforcement officers have another effective tool that has proved to be reliably consistent at catching folks who don't play by the rules and regulations. Dozens of volunteers from the Oregon Hunters Association have stepped forward to crack down on bullets and greed in the great outdoors. They team up with law officers to help catch game violators in the act and on camera. I recently observed the difference that volunteers can make when I joined Hoodenpyl and his team of officers and volunteers on a decoy operation. "First and foremost, we place the decoys in an area where we've had numerous complaints. Usually, it's a mainline road where lots of folks are going in or coming out of the woods. That location gives us a wide variety of people; not only campers, hikers, and hunters but oftentimes shooters. It gives us the most bang for the buck."

The officers know that their decoys may get shot full of holes but that's OK because a hundred yards away, Jim Kelly catches people who pull the trigger—on video. Kelly explained: "Some people want a deer or elk so bad, they're willing to do anything to get it—even break the law. They just get carried away." Kelly has been catching lawbreakers in the act with his video camera for the past fifteen hunting seasons. He told me that he'd "seen it all" during that time, from people who shoot from inside their vehicles, hunt without a license, or worse: "I have watched people nearly shoot their partner when they get out of the vehicle because of the way they handle a firearm. Sometimes gun safety goes out the window when hunters get 'Bull Fever,' and in fact, I've even seen people shoot through their vehicles."

Jim Kelly is a longtime member of the Oregon Hunters Association and donates his time and video equipment during the fall hunting seasons. In fact, Kelly is a big believer in volunteerism for the agency—he gives more than 500 hours of his time to help OSP each year. Why so many hours? "Oh, that's easy," said Kelly. "Each deer that's shot illegally out here costs the state of Oregon because of the time and effort that goes into managing the animals. Plus, when someone illegally kills a deer or elk, say at night, they've just stolen that animal from the legal hunter. It's all about protecting the resource and making sure people do the right thing."

Within just minutes of setting up the decoys, Kelly went to work as a lone vehicle cruised down the quiet forested back road; as the truck's headlamps lit up the decoys, the driver hit the brakes. He backed up, stopped, and stepped out of his vehicle—he knelt and fired off a quick round from his rifle. The decoys didn't move and the shooter realized his mistake and he attempted to flee the scene. He didn't get far as two OSP trucks converged on the rig.

The driver was questioned and we soon learned a sobering truth from OSP officer Ryan Howell:

Fake deer, nicknamed Scruffy, have been used by Oregon game officers since the 1980s to catch people who break hunting rules.

"He filled his deer tag yesterday so he was planning on putting his wife's tag on this deer—that's a problem." It is a problem because hunting for someone else is a clear violation of Oregon's hunting regulations. The spent shell casing was picked up—as an observer, Kelly compared his video of the events with the officer's observations and then two citations (one for the husband and one for the wife) were written by OSP game officer Doug Shuggart. He told me that volunteers like Kelly fill an important role by helping to stop bullets and greed: "When you go to court and you've got that video to show the judge, it can be really profound evidence. You can see the gun barrel slide out the window, see and hear the shot, and that lets both the judge and the jury see what actually took place with their own eyes."

Kelly told us that for him, he sees a simpler reason to be a volunteer: "To keep people honest. I believe in having a level playing field for all of the hunters—to make it fair for everybody. So I will keep lending a hand as long as I can and make sure that people play fair."

October

25

Salmon Watch

*M*y favorite sign of the seasonal transition from summer to fall is when big salmon muscle their way back to their home waters to spawn. Despite incredible odds that are stacked against them, the salmon continue a cycle of death and rebirth that is one for the ages. Consider the salmon's biology by the numbers: a large female chinook salmon will lay 3,000 to 5,000 eggs in the gravel. Biologists say the death toll on the eggs begins immediately for any number of reasons that include unfertilized eggs, silt or pollution that chokes off the eggs' oxygen absorption, water that is too warm, and a variety of predators.

When the baby fish do emerge from the gravel to search for food, they are immediately vulnerable and easy prey for

Chinook salmon, mottled black and gray, return to the Salmon River each October.

other fish, birds, and even mammals, and their numbers diminish even more. The tiny survivors spend upwards of 2 years in the freshwater habitat, growing larger and larger, and remain prime prey for other animals. The fish grow to 6 or 7 inches as they reach the smolt stage and migrate through the nutrient rich saltwater estuary. Here, the predator numbers continue to grow too, and it seems everything likes to eat the salmon throughout its entire life.

In the Pacific Ocean, the fish will travel hundreds—perhaps thousands—of miles for 2 to 3 more years and reach 30 pounds or more. But even in the vastness of the sea, they are susceptible to commercial harvest and larger finned

Salmon Watch offers school-aged children the chance to study salmon habitat in the field.

predators. At age 4, their biological alarm clock sounds and it is time to return to the exact place they were born and where the harvest toll continues to rise. The well-worn adage is so true for salmon: the odds are stacked against them. But for the chinook, it all works as nature intended: The adult salmon survivors number exactly two—one male and one female, out of all the thousands of eggs laid in the gravel 4 years earlier—that will continue their kind. It is an age-old story of death and rebirth that is a marvel. It's a remarkable journey and intriguing show and you can find some great spots to see the action. Many Oregon streams, like Eagle Creek in the Columbia River Gorge, bear out what the calendar says: summer has passed and now it is fall. The small creek near Bonneville Dam is often choked with chinook and coho salmon and it is a prime site to watch the fish.

The Salmon River near Welches, Oregon, also offers a fine spot for a salmon watch. Here, the chinook salmon are hard to miss—no longer gleaming silver, the big fish are mottled black and gray. They started life right here 4 years ago and that is a profound lesson not lost on Kirk Ordway's sixth-grade class. "I have been fortunate to join the Salmon Watch program for the past 4 years and it's huge with the kids; getting them out here and experiencing nature one on one," said Ordway. In fact, his group of youngsters are a part of 1,200 Portland-area students—ranging from middle school through high school—who will experience a Salmon Watch this fall thanks to the not-for-profit, Portland-based World Salmon Council. Ordway's watch actually began in his science class at Mt. Tabor Middle

School where the Salmon Watch program provides the curriculum, supplies, plus the cost of the field trip. The program even pays for a substitute teacher so Ordway can join his students in the field when Salmon Watch day arrives.

In the field, volunteer teacher Janet Davis (she is one of four volunteers assigned to each class) guided the young newcomers by teaching them scientific methods to measure the environment. Davis was retired when she learned that the Salmon Watch program needed volunteers, so she stepped up to lead her life in a new direction: "Students must be able to think systematically rather than 'Oh, I was told this, therefore it must be true.' They need a way to verify what they see and hear in a systematic way. Plus, I love the outdoors and wanted to be a part of it."

"Since the Salmon Watch program began more than 20 years ago, over 60,000 Oregon students have learned what salmon need to thrive," said Alyssa Thornburg. She is the Salmon Watch program manager and noted that, not surprisingly, it's what people need too—cold, clean water: "Salmon are so deeply characteristic of our region and yet kids grow up these days not knowing that—not knowing that we live so close to magnificent streams and that these salmon swim through here every season of the year. It's an important heritage that youngsters need to know so they can protect it." Mt. Tabor Middle School student Austin Larsen said that a day streamside, observing and learning, takes hold in a way the classroom can't: "We tested water quality and we ran some transect lines and quadrant lines in the forest to survey the vegetation. I have learned that salmon need specific conditions to live in, so the water needs to be a perfect range of temperatures or they won't survive. Well, I want to survive too, so it's important to know this information."

Ordway said that sort of understanding is important for his students, or anyone, who calls Oregon their home: "How often can you go around the city and see salmon running up a stream? You can't. How often can you walk through an old-growth forest? You can't! So the chance for us to come here, to an old-growth forest area along the Salmon River and bear witness to nature and its life cycles, it's a remarkable moment and you can't beat that."

25A Salmon River

Where: Located 20 miles east of Sandy, OR, off US Highway 26
Phone: Mt. Hood National Forest Headquarters: 503-668-1700
Web: www.worldsalmoncouncil.org
Watch the Episode: www.traveloregon.com/salmonwatch

Nehalem Falls

I 've a favorite adage that goes, "it is the journey that supports the destination." It is an insightful phrase that I have lived by whenever I travel throughout Oregon's great outdoors. Getting from this place to that is a journey to savor along a coastal byway that offers leaping salmon and spectacular fall colors—all within a 90-minute drive from Portland.

If the roadway flanking the Nehalem River has a number, I surely cannot find it on a map. Perhaps that's why I've such a love affair with this backdoor byway that takes a bit longer to get from this place to that. It breezes along nearly 30 miles beginning at a small whistle-stop village called Elsie (located on US Highway 26) and bounds down a narrow lane past limb-framed farms that cry "photo op" before it zips past softly rounded hillsides whose trees sport evidence of what calendars told us nearly a month ago: the seasons are changing.

The Nehalem River's tributaries also show you the changing times: some start as tiny, spring-fed trickles across spongy moss that later grow giant and creek-sized and where husky salmon have muscled their way back from salty sea to find their birth home in time to spawn. "It is so exciting, you just don't want to leave, can't stop watching them," said local photographer Don Best who was perched above popular Nehalem Falls at the Oregon Department of Forestry's Nehalem Falls Campground. (*Note*: the campground closes each September, but the trail to the falls remains open year round.)

Both chinook and coho salmon must muscle their way over the 10-foot Nehalem Falls to reach their spawning grounds.

Nehalem Falls drops more than 10 feet in a short, 20-yard series of churning drops that give salmon little choice but a gang-up approach to leaping for their lives. Best is an avid fan of the site and tries to capture the salmon show each fall. "I'll be here for hours trying to get that 'oooh-ahhh' shot," said the longtime outdoor photographer. "They jump high and they jump low and you never know where they'll show up. Plus, they're only in the air for half a second, so you don't always get them in the perfect shot. Some people take pictures underwater and they turn out really great. But to get them flying through the air is a different story; that's fun for me."

The water handsprings over unseen rocks through the falls while other river spots show off a distinct river's rhythm that provides a source of restoration for the life that grows here. The Nehalem River is always by your side on this scenic drive but you can enjoy a chance to break off from the roadway at Henry Rierson Spruce Run Campground. Abundant picnic tables complement a perfect riverside stop; rest and breathe in relaxation before you continue on your way. It is the colorful, wonderful show along this back road that I cherish most, where the big-leaf maple leaves, already mottled brown or gray, sometimes fall gently, gliding by the way. While other times, a breeze kicks up a blizzard and the leaves drop and stop on placid pools where barely a ripple marks the moment or the giant leaves collect and build in piles along the road providing a "drive-through" too inviting to refuse. So hurry here soon and then slow down on a back road without numbers that is one of the very best around.

25B Nehalem Falls Campground

Where: Located at Milepost 7 on Foss Road, Nehalem, OR 97131

Web: www.oregon.gov/odf

Phone: 503-842-2545

Watch the Episode: www.traveloregon.com/cruisingforcolor

26

Where Cars Don't Roll

*F*all has arrived in Oregon country with brilliant sunshine, perfect for a scenic adventure into remote territory that recalls the early days of life in Northeast Oregon—a time and place "where cars don't roll." The view from the Wallowa Lake Tramway near Wallowa Lake State Park is a marvel. It's a unique bird's-eye view of the surrounding countryside near Joseph, Oregon. Once you are atop Mt. Howard, glance to the Eagle Cap Wilderness or down to Wallowa Lake and you may never want to leave. Folks have felt that way about Wallowa and Union Counties for over a century—especially after the railroad made travel into the remote region far easier in the late 1800s.

The Eagle Cap Excursion pokes along at 10 miles an hour, so you will slow down and enjoy the 4-hour ride.

The people of Elgin, Oregon, make you feel right at home when you visit the Elgin Depot and step aboard the Eagle Cap Excursion Train. Dave Arnold is the railroad engineer at the controls of the GP7 diesel electric and he loves to brag: "I get the best seat in the house." Arnold said the train's engine produces 1500 horsepower and travels on the historic Joseph Branch Line built in 1884. "It is never the same trip," noted Arnold. "I think rolling along on a historic line that's still intact is exciting." The Eagle Cap Excursion Train is a one-of-a-kind rail trip where the Wallowa or Grande Ronde Rivers are always in view. It's also a railroad saved from ruin by local folks who believed there was value in holding on to their heritage—so they bought the railroad line in 2003. Stephen

Adams, a member of the Wallowa-Union County Railroad Authority, said that the scenic qualities are only a part of the railroad's appeal: "This is the only line in the country where a substantial amount of the track is in roadless terrain. That means this railroad is the only means for visitors to really explore this country—and we love visitors." The train runs a little over 40 miles and, while the scenery is spectacular and the nostalgia is impressive, the best part is that you have a chance to go where the cars don't roll.

Ann Warren is a volunteer for the weekend excursion rides and said that once guests come aboard the train, they've little choice but to slow down, take a deep breath, and savor the scenery: "Since the train moves along so slowly at 10 miles an hour, our trips last about 4 hours. It's all about being close to nature and seeing wildlife: bears, eagles, deer, and elk. Plus, you will turn off all your electronic devices because we have no cell phone coverage and not much radio. It's really nice that way." Local professional photographer Eric Valentine volunteers his time during the fall runs to tutor the folks who bring their cameras to capture the showy colors each October.

"You have so much natural beauty that really couldn't be any finer: the rising canyon walls of the Grande Ronde River are special and make you feel small, and then the river gives us something more to shoot, and the train's speed gives you an ever-changing setting that's breathtaking this time of year." It is a perfect getaway for folks who think they've seen it all in Oregon and yet recognize that the best travel surprises are those you least expect. "It's a fine trip for anyone who needs a change of pace," added Adams. The weekend trips have proven quite popular with locals and visitors alike. Reservations are advised.

26A Wallowa Lake Tramway

Where: 59919 Wallowa Lake Highway, Joseph, OR 97846

Web: www.wallowalaketramway.com

Phone: Summer: 541-432-5331; Winter: 503-781-4321

26B Elgin Depot

Where: 300 N. Eighth Street, Elgin, OR 97827

Web: eaglecaptrainrides.com

Phone: 800-323-7330

Watch the Episode: www.traveloregon.com/eaglecaptrain

27

Fern Ridge Wildlife Area

*O*ne of the most fascinating aspects of my news job has been covering the Northwest's dramatic environmental events and issues, particularly when severe weather affects us. The powerful periods of drought or deluge or blizzard or windstorm can have extreme effects upon our landscape and our lives, sometimes in heart-wrenching ways. For example, the infamous floods in 1996 and again in 2007 hit western Oregon with sudden one-two punches of rapid snowmelt and endless days of rain. The winter rain was not the typical gray-shaded drizzle either, but steady buckets of the stuff. Scores of forested canyons blew out a torrent of mud and debris into swollen, log-choked streams that washed out countless roads. Such has often been my beat in Tillamook County for weeks at a time. I can still vividly recall the devastation and the damage—millions of dollars' worth—not only to the land but also to the lives and livelihoods of small-town businesspeople who lost their shops and stores. Farmers lost their homes and barns, plus entire herds of milk-producing cows and other livestock that couldn't escape the fast-rising floodwater.

Several years of drought in 2001, 2013, and more recently in 2014 were just as ruinous for people who depend upon water for their farms and businesses. Droughts have prompted unusual wildlife behavior too. In fact, I recall well that in 2001 the parched Willamette Valley at the normally wet world of Fern Ridge Reservoir in Lane County, a bird species arrived that hadn't been seen there in more than half a century: white pelicans! Stumps, mudflats, and low, low water created a scene largely devoid of people on Fern Ridge Reservoir that summer. The lake shrunk to about half its normal 9,000 acres, so the contrast to previous summers was startling. Usually the reservoir is a boater's playground, but the drought meant no more fill-ups at the county boat marina, where dozens of

White pelicans cruise above Fern Ridge Reservoir on 6-foot wingspans.

wooden boat docks were stacked atop each other like cordwood, and popular swimming holes were transformed into lonely beachfronts.

Yet the wildlife adapted just fine. Shorebirds still probed the muck of the shoreline for food while ospreys soared high overhead. Even though the reservoir dropped to 10 feet below its normal height, many hiking trails, usually swampy adventures at best, were actually bone-dry and easier to follow. Such were the conditions I found when I traveled down the Fisher Butte Trail at the southeast corner of the reservoir, where a short trek to the shoreline put me and my partner, Wayne Morrow, a now-retired biologist with the Oregon Department of Fish and Wildlife, just a short distance from the rare presence of about three dozen white pelicans preening and resting on a treeless sand island. "My gosh, Wayne," I whispered, "pelicans are really huge." He smiled, nodded, and in a hushed tone offered, "Oh yeah—they are unmistakable. You know, it's so neat to see them here. Last time was just after World War II. There are so few people around this summer that the birds may find the reservoir much more appealing. Plus, there's more exposed sandbar, which is ideal for the birds to rest on."

Pelicans weigh up to 20 pounds with wingspans reaching 7 or 8 feet. They are a brilliant bright white, so they stand out from quite a distance. White pelicans are usually found only in the Malheur or Klamath regions, but the drought brought them much farther north and west than normal. As many as forty were spotted on the lake where shallow water, mudflats, and a steady diet of freshwater clams created their ideal habitat. Morrow suggested that the pelicans may have rediscovered the historic habitat and he wouldn't be surprised if they return for many summers to come. And in fact, they have. If you travel the Fisher Butte Trail, you may see them too.

This seasonal reservoir is one of Oregon's most popular, with over a million visitors per year. Built by the Corps of Engineers in 1941, the Fern Ridge project includes about 12,000 acres (more than 19 square miles) and was built for flood control and irrigation. Popular for sailing, powerboating, waterskiing, and swimming, Fern Ridge Reservoir offers several park sites for day use and for overnight camping. Two public marinas and the Eugene Yacht Club host several sailing regattas each summer. Wildlife viewing opportunities are abundant, and refuges comprise a large part of extensive adjoining wetlands.

Approximately 5,000 acres on the east and south sides of the reservoir are leased by the Corps to the Oregon Department of Fish and Wildlife as the Fern Ridge Wildlife Area, and are one of the best places to spot a bald eagle or two or three. Kevin Roth, the wildlife area's assistant manager, says these wetlands, ponds, and sloughs and upland areas "are a fine place to start—not just to view the waterfowl that use the wetlands and ponds but the raptors too. Our number one goal is to provide food, water, and sanctuary for wintering birds and at times we're like a magnet. You will see several species in just one visit." Roth added that his best tip to spot birds of prey is to simply "drive around. Especially the back roads of farmland. Stop and look often, especially scan the trees, chances are you will see an eagle or a hawk—they are that common and without leaves on the trees, easier to spot this time of year."

---

27 Fern Ridge Wildlife Area

Where: 26969 Cantrell Road, Eugene, OR 97402

Web: www.dfw.state.or.us

Phone: 541-935-2591

28

Downtown Salmon

*I*f you spend much time traveling across Oregon in October, you will begin to see and feel the early signs of the changing seasons. For me, one of the surest signs of transition from summer to fall is the many places you might cast a lure or drift bait for salmon along coastal Oregon. There's a unique fishery on the southern coastline at Coos Bay where a community's determined effort and strong commitment has made a difference in restoring a nearly extinct salmon run.

Coos Bay's waterfront streetlights sparkle when you join longtime fishing guide Rick Howard on a first light fishing trip in October. It takes only a few minutes of travel across the smooth estuary in Howard's comfortable 25-foot boat to reach the salmon-rich water that is marked by fog-shrouded silhouettes. They are fishermen and with their fishing rods bent over double and their nets flying high, they are a sure sign that eager salmon are on the bite.

If you want to catch one, noted Howard, you must prepare a "plug cut" herring for bait; thread it onto hooks that are tied to a 5-foot leader that's secured to a brass swivel with a 4-ounce lead sinker. The tackle and terminal gear must be trolled just off the estuary bottom with the falling tide. Or, if you lack the skill and experience, sign up to join Howard for a day on the bay. Then you can watch in awe as he deftly handles his boat through watercraft traffic and prepares the baited rods for you and your fishing partners.

"Fishing at the right speed and at the right depth are key points," noted Howard with a knowing smile. "You must also make sure the baits are clean and don't have human scent on them." This is autumn fishing on Coos Bay, where the downtown salmon run has begun. Howard is quick and efficient at catching them, relying on skills born of a lifetime of guiding fishermen across these waters. "Basically, this is where Coos River starts," said Howard. "These fall chinook

Each October, lucky anglers can land a trophy like this 30-pound chinook on Coos Bay.

salmon are fresh from the sea and they are coming right here—across the 10,000-acre estuary in front of town. They linger here a bit to make sure this is their home water and it is probably the most productive spot to be fishing at this time of year."

Tom Rumreich is an Oregon Department of Fish and Wildlife (ODFW) biologist and he agreed that the downtown Coos Bay salmon fishery is one of the most productive in the state. But then, for the past 30 years, he has helped to build it that way. Rumreich helps guide the local ODFW "STEP," or "Salmon and Trout Enhancement Program," that has uniquely brought together thousands of local volunteers, businesses, and even schoolchildren to raise money, build hatcheries, and do the heavy lifting to bring back a basin-wide fall chinook salmon run. "Our STEP project for fall salmon is unique from the standpoint of how many people work for the common goal of putting more fish here for everyone," noted the fishery biologist. "There's great pride in that fact." There's good reason to be proud when you consider the Coos River watershed's legacy of poor salmon habitat—habitat that was stripped from the streams by old logging practices called "splash damming." In a splash dam operation, temporary wooden dams collected the logs and then, in a heartbeat, the dams were broken open to quickly move the big wood downstream to reach Coos Bay's lumber mills.

The splash dam era began in the late 1800s and didn't end until 1958. Rumreich said the damage to salmon runs was devastating and long lasting: "Biologists prior to me said you could walk up many Coos River watershed streams and rivers and not find a 5-gallon bucket of gravel in any of them. In fact, some biologists back then reported that the Coos River fall chinook went from 100,000 fish strong to extinction." But today it's a different story, thanks to an ongoing hatchery program that finds more than 3,000 STEP volunteers who raise more than 2 million baby salmon each year. The adult volunteers work with schoolchildren to help capture the adult fish, spawn them, and then each spring, volunteers remove the adipose fin that marks each fish's hatchery origin.

The Coos Bay STEP project is not only a hatchery program, but funds and provides manpower for river habitat restoration projects too. The varied projects help restore the rivers so that wild salmon get a boost to increase natural salmon spawning production. Eric Farm, former president of the Bay Area Chamber of Commerce, added that the projects help further environmental education for local students: "Our kids hold the big chinook in their hands, they spawn the fish, clip the adipose fins off the smolt, and send them down the raceway. Those experiences will stick with them the rest of their lives. Our community put their hands into this project and now, after 30 years, we are reaping the rewards of that effort."

Howard said the rewards are shared with thousands of sport anglers each fall. He said the last year more than 11,000 fall chinook were caught by anglers who spent nearly 3.5 million dollars in the local community. Rumreich added it's no surprise that the project's community support has been widespread: "People in our community benefit, not only by catching the fish, but by the economic boost that comes from fishing gear sales, motel rooms, restaurant meals, and so much more. It's so amazing to see all of these people out here enjoying themselves in a great place, a great community—it's a uniquely Oregon experience."

28 Coos Bay

Where: On US Highway 101, about 50 miles south of Florence, OR
Web: www.dfw.state.or.us/fish/STEP
Phone: ODFW STEP: 541-888-5515

Rick Howard Guide Service

Web: www.howard5.net/rhguide
Phone: 541-347-3280

Watch the Episode: www.traveloregon.com/downtownsalmon

November

29

A Stroll Along South Slough

*I*f there is a "Shangri-La" on Oregon's coastline, I may have found it along the southern coast near Coos Bay. If you make the journey, you'll discover an off-the-beaten path location with unique sights and sounds at the South Slough National Estuarine Research Reserve. The Cape Arago Highway skirts a lonesome and lovely section of the southern Oregon coast, and you quickly find it's a road once taken that you'll never want to leave. It leads you past so many intriguing sights that you may well wonder, Why have I never come this way before?

Fourteen miles southwest of Coos Bay, drop in at Sunset Bay State Park and

There are more than 5,000 acres of land and water to explore at South Slough Estuary.

meet Oregon State Parks Manager Preson Phillips, who told me: "It's one of those trails that just keeps beckoning you on—it's just a matter of how much you want to hike or do at the time." Make time to wander Sunset Bay State Park, a jewel of a campground that offers 139 sites for tent, trailer, or RV—plus eight yurts. People who come to camp enjoy a spectacular beachfront that seems framed for the movies—it has been a special destination park since 1942. If you own a spirit of adventure, you'll no doubt relish the hiking trail that leads little more than a mile to nearby Cape Arago State Park. Many visitors are surprised to find a front row seat of sorts—a wooden balcony that overlooks Shell Island.

A sprawling, multilevel wooden deck offers visitors a fine perch to see the estuary.

Marty Giles, owner of an ecotourism business called Wavecrest Discoveries, is often on hand to explain the behavior of hundreds of seals and sea lions that just plain loaf across the rocky island and Simpson Reef: "Shell Island is a fine place for them to haul out and rest for a while. You really need to come on up and see this show." You will want to make time to travel 5 miles farther up the Seven Devils Road to visit a piece of Oregon coastal paradise that's been preserved since 1974.

The South Slough National Estuarine Research Reserve offers a visitor center that introduces you to the area with varied multimedia and hands-on exhibits. Together, the displays put you in touch with a rare piece of Oregon coastal environment according to the center's Deborah Rudd: "It is undisturbed, it is not developed, and you do have more interaction with wildlife here. It's quiet. It's peaceful. And you can picture what life was like many years ago across this southern branch of greater Coos Bay." There are more than 5,000 acres in South Slough Reserve—approximately 1,000 of those are the slough itself, then the rest is protected upland forest or marshland. There is plenty of elbow room to explore at South Slough Reserve and there are plenty of trails that take you out and about. One of my favorites is called the Hidden Creek Trail—a little over a mile in length with a wonderful wooden boardwalk that takes you out over a wetland area where the freshwater creek meets the sea.

In addition, there are many stunning views along the trail, including those from atop a two-level deck that looks across a marsh area to the Winchester Arm of the slough. The reserve is open throughout the calendar year, but South Slough Reserve education director Tom Gaskill says some seasons offer unique surprises for the hearty traveler: "I'm a birder, so for me this time of year in fall is the beginning of the most exciting part of the season. We have flocks of waterfowl that pass through here and a lot of the overwintering forest birds too—there are many species that we never see here during the summer, so it's exciting in the winter months to see some of these migratory species that spend summers in Alaska and Canada, but they're here for the winter."

"It is a beautiful place whatever season you come to visit," added Rudd. "You will be amazed and it will be worth your effort to come find us."

29A South Slough National Estuarine Research Reserve

Where: 61907 Seven Devils Road, Charleston, OR 97420
Web: www.oregon.gov
Phone: 541-888-5558

29B Sunset Bay State Park

Where: 89814 Cape Arago Highway, Coos Bay, OR 97420
Web: www.oregonstateparks.org
Phone: 541-888-3778

29C Cape Arago State Park

Where: At the end of Cape Arago Highway, Coos Bay, OR
Web: www.oregonstateparks.org
Phone: 541-888-3778

Watch the Episode: www.traveloregon.com/southslough

30

Sauvie Island Sandhills

$\mathcal{E}$ach fall, a feathery invasion drops into Oregon's fields and wetlands as a quarter million Canada geese arrive on fixed wings with a rowdy chorus. At the Sauvie Island Wildlife Area, look closely and listen carefully for another bird species that stands head and shoulders above the crowd. Sandhill cranes are hard to miss and it's not just their 3-foot height and 6-foot wingspan, noted assistant wildlife area manager, Dan Marvin: "This is the spot! As far as opportunities to view sandhill cranes go in the Willamette Valley—this is it."

It's not only their distinct size, but adult cranes also have a striking red color across their faces. According to Gary Ivey, Oregon's sandhill crane expert: "Adults have a bright red crown—a bright red forehead really—and the chicks don't have that. In fact, the chicks look a lot paler in the face." There's an even more distinct feature. He said that the sandhill sounds are unlike anything you've ever heard: "Well, it's kind of a loud trumpet that has kind of a trill to it. You can hear it from a long way off and the flocks use it as a contact call. Often, when they are migrating you will hear that call, even when they're almost invisible so high up. Once you hear the sound you never forget it."

The big birds fly to Sauvie Island from as far away as southeast Alaska and British Columbia and they spend the win-

Sandhill cranes put on an entertaining display during their mating season.

ter lounging across the refuge grounds. The peak of their arrival is mid-October when up to 4,000 birds show up on Sauvie Island. Most continue flying farther south, but approximately a quarter of them stay here all winter long. The best time to see them is during the early morning or late afternoon when birds are actively feeding in harvested grain fields. Be sure to bring good optics too, either binoculars or a spotting scope; each will make a big difference enjoying the view of the birds.

The "view" to all of Oregon's wildlife has recently improved, according to Rick Hargrave, a spokesperson for the Oregon Department of Fish and Wildlife. He said that a recent survey showed nearly 2 million people spend more than a billion dollars each year to travel and watch Oregon wildlife: "We knew right then that we needed to get something out to the public to make viewing a little easier and to highlight the wildlife that the department oversees and manages." The new interactive Oregon Wildlife Viewing Map helps you see more of Oregon's fish and wildlife species. It is a Google-based map that details 235 great places to see wildlife in the state. You can discover where to see bald eagles or sage grouse or migrating snow geese. It points you to good sites to view Oregon's largest mammals including migrating gray whales or high desert antelope or Rocky Mountain elk.

Hargrave said the map's sites reach into each corner of the state: "The state agency manages fish and wildlife for the people of Oregon," added Hargrave. "We want people to understand the connections between wildlife viewing, conservation, and the habitat. Without an emphasis on all of those, you're not going to see the variety of wildlife that we have in this great state." You've plenty of time to enjoy the sandhill show and hear their haunting calls. Sauvie Island Wildlife Area is their home through winter; the colorful birds return north to their breeding and nesting grounds in April.

---

30 Sauvie Island Wildlife Area

Where: 18330 NW Sauvie Island Road, Portland, OR 97231

Web: www.dfw.state.or.us

Phone: 503-621-3488

Oregon Wildlife Viewing Map

Web: www.dfw.state.or.us/maps

Watch the Episode: www.traveloregon.com/sandhillcranes

31

Focus on Nature

*Y*ou are apt to find me off the beaten path much of the year and more often than not it will be where the asphalt turns to gravel. Recently, I laced up hiking boots and grabbed my camera to join a pro photographer who has made a career with a "focus on nature." Many believe that great adventures only happen in distant, far-off lands. But not Nancy J. Smith. She prefers prowling her home state's soggy trails for sneak peeks at nature—like the short hike into University Falls in the Tillamook State Forest. "Oh, there's so much to see in here . . . even the gorgeous white bark on these alder trees is just beautiful," exclaimed Smith with a broad smile. As she clutched her well-used Canon cam-

era, she added, "I love what I do—can you tell?" It is easy to fall in love with University Falls; the trail rises and falls on a short half-mile trek before dropping steeply to a viewpoint at the base of the falls on the north side of Elliott Creek.

Elliott Creek is a small drainage so the falls won't flow nearly as powerfully in the summer as they do in the winter. That's especially true following a heavy rain when the fully-charged creek creates a scenic 55-foot falls that is more akin to a silky wedding veil draped over a wall of rugged basalt. It results in a stunning show for photographers. Nancy's husband, Bert Olheiser, was by her side

University Falls offers a lacy curtain of foam and spray so bring your camera and capture the stunning scene.

Nancy J. Smith doesn't mind getting her feet wet to get the "perfect shot" for her annual calendars.

on an otherwise gray-shaded, drizzly day. He carried the gear and shielded the camera lens from the light, but constant, rainfall. "I'll help her get to the spot and get the equipment set up," said Olheiser, "and then I stand back and say, 'Nancy, work your magic.'" Nancy's camera magic often means getting her feet wet in water that's cold as ice. "Sometimes I get in the creek and sometimes I balance my tripod and my feet on the slippery rocks along the bank," said Smith. "I do what I can to make the scene look good."

Smith has not only made Oregon "look good" for nearly 27 years, but she has captured beautiful, breathtaking, iconic scenes across the entire state and drawn a dedicated following too. She prides herself on capturing a scene that puts you in the spot, fills you with pride for Oregon's wonder, and puts a smile on your face. But here's the thing—the camera she has used throughout her career isn't digital but film. "This Canon film camera is the one I've always used for my business; it's my workhorse for sure and I love it. Some people may think that's an old wave thing and maybe I'm keeping the tradition of photography alive, but it seems to work for me. I love the color saturation from film; it's beautiful and people love it." People really love her "Majestic Pacific Northwest Calendars" too. They have been a staple of Smith's photographic repertoire since 1990.

In fact, her photos have been judged best-of-show alongside entries from *National Geographic* and *Arizona Highways*. It's pretty heady stuff for a woman who grew up in the countryside near her hometown of Gresham, Oregon, and fondly recalls childhood days of catching crawdads from nearby creeks: "It was my playground and I fell in love with the outdoors at a very early age." As Smith approaches her sixth decade in the Oregon outdoors, she said that she has never lost that thrill that comes from exploring new places. Her youthful exuberance comes from discovering something new each time she goes out and that keeps her young at heart too. "She does have a lot of energy," admitted Olheiser. "I need a cup of coffee or two to start moving in the morning but she jumps out of bed going 50 miles an hour. It's her positive and open view of life that's so inspiring. She really appreciates her time here."

Judging from the sheer joy she found at University Falls, Smith shows no signs of slowing. She admitted that her time in the outdoors is never about the destination, but what she might find in the small details along the journey. She added that insatiable curiosity keeps her on the trail of photographic adventures and the trail of her life. "It really is the reason I get so excited," said Smith. "My best adventures are the 'along-the-way' discoveries—the small things—and life is like that too. If we just take the time to enjoy the journey, it's so much better."

31 University Falls Trailhead, Tillamook State Forest

Where: About 3 miles from State Highway 6; follow signs for University Falls Trailhead

Web: www.oregon.gov/odf

Phone: Oregon Department of Forestry, Forest Grove District Office: 503-357-2191

Nancy J. Smith Photography

Web: www.focusonpd.com

Phone: 503-658-4408

Watch the Episode: www.traveloregon.com/focusonnature

Afoot and Afloat on the Nestucca River

 ach November as the holiday season kicks into high gear, many of us may find that our lives are speeding by at a shattering pace. I say take a deep breath and savor a place where you can go with the flow and follow a tide meant for the quiet times along the Little Nestucca River in Tillamook County. The waterway cuts a beeline through the Nestucca Bay National Wildlife Refuge (NBNWR) and the trip is so easy anyone can try on a river paddle with local guides called Kayak Tillamook who cater to beginners.

Paddlers dress warm when they join Kayak Tillamook's November guided tour of Nestucca Bay.

"The paddle trip flows right next to the forest and through the wildlife refuge," said guide Marcus Hinz. "As you paddle out toward the bay you quickly forget there's anything else around you except the wildlife." You may see bald eagles, red-tailed hawks, osprey, deer, elk, beavers, river otters, and more—in fact, the bird life is remarkable. Be sure to dress warm, and in layers to accommodate your level of activity. Avoid cotton. Don't forget a rain jacket, cap, and gloves. A life jacket is provided and it is mandatory on a trip where safety comes first. "When you're paddling in a kayak, you're much less intrusive than a car," added Hinz. "You get pretty close to the Canada geese and other waterfowl because [in a small boat] they're not as frightened away from you."

Nestucca Bay National Wildlife Refuge is also a place where you can leave the paddles behind and take a stroll along the refuge trail, just off Cannery Hill Road, that meanders across the heart of the refuge. US Fish and Wildlife Biologist Roy Lowe said that NBNWR was established in 1991 to protect Canada geese that migrate to coastal Oregon from Alaska. "You are missing something special if you don't come up and take a look," noted Lowe. "While you may drive by the site on Coastal Highway 101 and see this ridge, folks should really take a drive up here. The refuge is spectacular." It is also a refuge that's been successful for wildlife protection. Lowe added that in the late '80s, up to 1,000 geese wintered across the refuge marsh and pastures. Now, nearly 10,000 geese show up here from November through March.

The stunning viewpoint atop the wooden deck offers a breathtaking panorama that reaches from the mountains to the sea. "Sunset is spectacular, sunrise too," noted Lowe. "In fact, if you come here once that doesn't mean it's going to be the same the next time—it can be spectacular anytime depending upon the conditions." Hinz added that the Little Nestucca River is a timeless and easygoing adventure: "It really is the best of both worlds because you're seeing the land from the water as opposed to seeing the water from the land, so it is a much more intimate experience and you really feel like you're in nature." In addition to the NBNWR trip, there are more than 800 miles of water trails in Tillamook County that reach across rivers, estuaries, and sloughs. There's even a series of maps to guide your way called Tillamook County Water Trails.

32 Nestucca Bay National Wildlife Refuge
Where: 7000 Christensen Road, Cloverdale, OR 97112
Web: www.fws.gov/oregoncoast/nestuccabay
Phone: 541-867-4550

Kayak Tillamook
Web: kayaktillamook.com
Phone: 503-866-4808

Tillamook County Water Trails
Web: www.tbnep.org/water-trails

Watch the Episode: www.traveloregon.com/nestuccawildlife

December

33

Oregon's Dungeness Crab

*W*hen you're lucky enough to go fishing with a good friend who knows the water well, you're sure to learn something new. That's especially true when the Columbia River is under your keel to carry you toward new adventure. Steve Fick first explored the Columbia River estuary as a kid, so he knows his way around the vast waterway where the river meets the sea. We left the snug harbor of Hammond, Oregon, near Astoria and slowly motored the short distance downriver to an area just off Clatsop Beach. Fick had prepared five large crab pots or traps with varied baits—a strategy he often uses so to "see what the crabs prefer."

Fresh Dungeness crabs are Oregon's most valuable seafood commodity.

Sometimes he'll use turkey legs, chicken wings, shad or salmon carcasses, even a can of tuna for crab bait. Anyone say "lunchtime?" "Oh yes, a can of tuna fish is perfect bait," exclaimed Fick. "All you do is perforate the can so that the scent comes out. You can also buy canned sardines or mackerel too; both work well. As long as they have a high oil content, it seems to fish well; the scent is what draws the crab into the pot."

Each Oregon crabber must carry an Oregon Department of Fish and Wildlife Shellfish License. Each crabber is allowed to use up to three crab pots. (We timed our trip to fish our traps during the last hour of the incoming tide and then through the high slack

Drawn by the scent of fresh bait, Dungeness crabs climb into the crab pot but they cannot get back out.

tide period that's often the best crabbing time.) Fick said it's the safest time to crab in the estuary: "There is no reason to be out here on the ebb tide—that's the outgoing tide and things can go from bad to worse in a heartbeat. It can be the most dangerous part of the tide cycle and this river can change so fast. You just don't take chances out here."

Fick said that each trap should "soak" for 15 to 20 minutes. That allows enough time for the crabs to locate the bait and enter the pot. Each crabber is allowed a dozen male crabs apiece and in Oregon they must be 5¾ inches across the back. Females are protected to preserve the breeding population of crabs. A crab gauge or other measuring device is essential gear since some crabs miss the mark by only a fraction of an inch. Fick and I soon had our hands full of fresh crabs, but truth was the trap made the catching easy—and it turns out, the crab pot is "All Oregon!"

At the Airport Crab Pot Company in Warrenton, they have rolled the steel into rings, welded the weights in place, wrapped the rings in rubber, and woven the steel mesh into crab pots since 1948. "Building a crab pot—one that will fish well—is a science," said company owner Vern Lamping. His wife, Lisa Lamping, added, "They really got it right way back then—there are little things you can do, but for the most part there isn't a better way to catch crab." Lisa is right. Dungeness crabbing dates to the earliest days of commercial fishing in Oregon's offshore waters. It was a profitable way to make a living for many commercial fishermen during the slack times between salmon runs.

Inside Oregon's only sport and commercial crab pot manufacturing company, you soon see that the heritage of the business is alive and well. Gene Elliott, Paul Shaw, and Mike Gill collectively own more than a century of experience building pots the old-fashioned way—with their hands. They "hand knit" each pot using stainless steel wire to make each pot's top, bottom, and sides. "Get ready to bleed," noted Gill with a chuckle. "It is really hard on the hands." The 18-guage stainless steel wire requires tough, quick hands and a sharp eye to knit the mesh just right. "You have to hold the meshes at exactly the same size," said Shaw. "So, you really must stay focused on the work all of the time." Elliott added: "I've been at this for more than 37 years, just like these fellas, but I was also a fisherman so I made and repaired my own gill nets. I was already familiar with the knitting techniques before I started working on crab pots."

Lisa Lamping explained that it's all piecework so each weaver must be accurate and speedy if they wish to make money: "Each of these men is able to consistently weave the mesh accurately; the meshes must be about 2 inches wide. It's very old-school and it hasn't changed much in a hundred years."

Down at the dock is where the work pays off. Oregon's Dungeness crab harvest is the state's most valuable seafood. Last year, the coast-wide catch was worth nearly 50 million dollars. "It's an economic component that fills a big void from December to March for many fishermen," said Fick, who owns Fishhawk Fisheries in Astoria. "Families live here and the infrastructure of support—like the crab pot businesses or the marine supply stores—all of that business stays in our community and it is key to the viability of rural life along the Oregon coast."

33 Clatsop Beach

Where: From the mouth of the Columbia River south to Tillamook Head

Phone: Oregon Department of Fish and Wildlife: 503-325-2462 or 541-867-4741

Airport Crab Pot Company

Where: 770 SE 13th Place, Warrenton, OR 97146

Web: airportcrabpot.com

Phone: 503-338-8778

Watch the Episode: www.traveloregon.com/wintercrab

My Favorite Crab Recipe

Stuffed Crab Sandwich

*I*t is also a lot of fun to catch your own crabs and then head to the kitchen where Steve Fick shared a favorite recipe called a Stuffed Crab Sandwich. "You can do a lot of different things with crab meat," said Fick. "You can make a chowder, fritters, salads, sandwiches—so many different things. You can mix it with fettuccine, other seafood, so it's very versatile."

Fick cut four sandwich rolls in half to make eight sandwiches. He then mixed 1 cup of grated Swiss cheese with 2 cups of crab and added 1 teaspoon each of Worcestershire sauce and lemon pepper before he mixed in 1 cup of mayo and half a cup of sliced olives. The mixture was stuffed into each half of a hollowed-out sandwich roll. Fick then spread a generous amount of grated Parmesan cheese across the top of each roll and slid the tray of sandwiches into a 375°F oven for 7 to 10 minutes. "This is a filling dinner," he noted. "You need to be in the mood for something rich and robust. It works well on a cold winter's night."

It was a perfect way to round out our crabbing adventure and bring the day's activity full circle: from the estuary to the dining table. Interestingly, Fick added that 80 percent of the crab is caught and shipped to market each December, the first month of the season—it's also the time when prices for the seafood are at their lowest. Plus, even if you don't sportfish for crab, the annual commercial crabbing season provides fresh Oregon Dungeness in your local grocery. As we enjoyed a very filling seafood dinner, I asked Fick what he liked most about the adventure that's just off his front doorstep: "Oh, it's simple to do and everyone can be involved in it. It's easy to catch a dozen crabs per person with lots of action for kids. And—you never really know until you pull the pot up what you got, and that is fun."

34

White River Wildlife Area and White River Falls State Park

*B*ack road byways are the best when they lead you down trails toward Oregon's secret hideaways. The east side of Mt. Hood offers two hideaways for the price of one getaway and each feels a million miles away from city hubbub and noise. Take to the open road and discover an easy-to-reach high desert point of view with a wildlife area and a state park waiting for you. It's little more than a 90-minute drive from Portland to explore Oregon's White River Wildlife Area.

It's a place where you may soon discover that back-road adventures are the very best when they let you enjoy a sneak peek at nature. There are nearly 30,000 acres of refuge that reach across more than 20 miles of terrain and provide an eastern point of view to the mountain. Josh Moulton, the White River Wildlife Area manager, noted, "We're a bit off the beaten path for sure; tucked out here in the oaks and pines at about 2,100 feet in elevation. You soon see, it's a different sort of wildlife area."

The White River Wildlife Area was established in the 1950s to keep wintering deer and a growing elk herd up in the Cascade Mountain foothills rather than down on neighboring farmlands. "A winter feeding program continues to serve the wildlife, both deer and elk," added Moulton. "We begin feeding in early December at designated stations throughout the refuge and the animals pretty much tell us by their behavior when to stop. We plant alfalfa in a nearby field each year and the deer love that. It's giving visitors a bit more reliable opportunity for viewing the deer herds too—the herds can reach several hundred strong in the winter."

Moulton added that the eastside view to Mt. Hood is a surprise for visitors: "We're less than 20 miles as the crow flies and while many of my friends in the valley say, 'You should see our view of Mt. Hood,' I have to chuckle because you really should see it from this side too. It really shines from up here." Above the nearby burg of Tygh Valley, an overlook provides a glimpse to the namesake White River and marks a route that pioneers followed in the great migration across Oregon to reach the Willamette Valley. There are several lakes and ponds but a short cast away where boating and fishing can be enjoyed. "Many folks have weekend or summer homes at Pine Hollow Reservoir and nearby Rock Creek Reservoir," said Moulton. "People come for the fishing—trout fishing. It's easy access for the kids too; no steep banks."

From Tygh Valley, you can strike out farther east on a short 4-mile drive along State Highway 216 to another secret hideaway where the White River plunges over a basalt shelf. White River Falls State Park offers a sprawling greenway with scattered picnic tables at a day-use site that opens each spring. You'll be drawn to explore the rugged quarter-mile trail that takes you riverside where you discover something more. A complicated system of pipes and flumes diverted water from above the falls down into a powerhouse and where electricity-producing turbines generated power for the region from 1910 to 1960.

The Dalles Dam construction and completion led to the White River project's demise and it shut down in the '60s. For obvious safety reasons, Oregon State Parks does not want visitors inside the old powerhouse building that is falling in upon itself. "Keep Out" signs on the shuttered building make that message clear, so observe the signs as you explore the riverside scenery. Do not forget a camera when you hike this path for the photo ops are numerous and stunning: of the river, the canyon, and the powerful White River Falls where two plunge pool falls drop more than 90 feet in dramatic fashion. The park is a popular picnicking, hiking, and fishing retreat for visitors who wish to dip their toes in this corner of the greater Deschutes River corridor. The White River Wildlife Area and White River Falls State Park offer easy-to-reach high desert escapes—for scenery, history, and relaxation.

34A White River Wildlife Area
Where: 78430 Dodson Road, Tygh Valley, OR 97063
Web: www.dfw.state.or.us
Phone: 541-544-2126

34B White River Falls State Park
Where: Along State Highway 216 about 5 miles east of Tygh Valley, OR
Web: www.oregonstateparks.org
Phone: 541-739-2322

Watch the Episode: www.traveloregon.com/whiteriver

35

A Friend to the Critters

One sure way to get to know the Oregon outdoors is to get to know its wildlife a bit better, so I caught up with a wildlife champion and friend to the critters at a place you can visit. Dave Siddon has walked the talk of helping sick and injured wildlife for more than 30 years. He owns and manages Wildlife Images near Grants Pass in Southern Oregon. Throughout his lifetime of study and hands-on practice, Siddon has come to know hawks and eagles and vultures and scores of other sharp-eyed birds of prey very well.

For many years he was a fixture at the Oregon Zoo—even started their raptor program. Twelve years ago he decided to go home to Wildlife Images

Dave Siddon cares for varied wildlife—from bears to cougars to golden eagles.

and follow his father's life's work rehabilitating sick or injured animals and educating folks. His father, Dave Siddon Sr., was a well-known figure in the wildlife rehabilitation world. He opened the clinic in 1981 following his own passion for helping cougars and eagles and bears get well and get back to the wild. Dave Sr. passed away in 1996 following a battle with cancer, and his son promised to dedicate his life to the center's most important mission. "When my father was dying of cancer he came to me and said, 'Would you consider leaving the zoo and making sure my place doesn't die along with me?' and how do you say no to that? So I came down here and dedicated my life to making sure this place continues to do the good work it does."

Dave Siddon Jr. was well prepared for the challenge. He worked for SeaWorld where he trained sea lions and dolphins, he worked at the Oregon Zoo for a dozen years, and he has blazed his own trail into the world of wildlife rehabilitation. Wildlife Images spreads across 24 acres offering wildlife viewing opportunities at every turn: perhaps a fox, a bobcat, a large brown bear, and especially the wildlife that fly. Siddon said that some animals come to Wildlife Images from would-be pet owners who realize too late that some critters just don't make good house pets. The center receives and treats over 2,500 animals annually, and approximately 90 percent of those that survive their initial injuries are returned to the wild. The organization's clinic, nature center, and animal-holding facilities are adjacent to Oregon's famous Wild and Scenic Rogue River, which serves as an excellent location for wildlife release.

Each year thousands of visitors tour the center to see animals ranging from grizzly bears to mountain lions to small arctic foxes and even tiny hummingbirds. As we strolled past display cages containing coyotes, a badger, porcupines, red foxes, and others, Siddon pointed out with pride the close-up opportunities that visitors enjoy at an open-air exhibit for bald eagles, turkey vultures, and ravens. As we walked into the small building, Siddon reached over and lifted a large metal window. The opening looked out to a grassy area, dotted with many small native plants and towering trees jutting to the sky.

A fine mesh net draped over the entire scene and prevented the birds from leaving the grounds. "Perfect perches," I noted as I admired the very natural setting. Siddon then shared more of his father's vision and passion: "It was my father's real dream to put together a facility for the bald eagles and other raptors where people can see them without wire and obstructions. They're such beautiful and majestic birds, you'd like to see them in some sort of situation that mimics what you'd see in the wild." Wildlife Images offers unique educational opportunities to schools, organizations, and the general public and conducts tours 6 days a week year-round. Reservations are required, and the facility is closed most national holidays. You can wander with a tour and learn more about the remarkable people that help Oregon wildlife motivated by Siddon's simple yet powerful belief: "If you don't have wildlife it's not a good place to be."

35 Wildlife Images

Where: 11845 Lower River Road, Grants Pass, OR 97526

Web: www.wildlifeimages.org

Phone: 541-476-0222

Watch the Episode: www.traveloregon.com/wildlifeimages

36

Backyard Birding

*I*f you like to feed wild birds, join the club; it's not only popular, but it's easy to do. The trouble is if you don't feed the right seeds you could do more environmental harm than good. In fact, backyard bird feeders can draw scores of species close to our homes each winter, so what you put out for the birds can also make a difference to your feeding success. Portland Audubon Society's Karen Munday recently said that some seed is bad for birds because some feed mixes contain nonnative weed seeds: "The last thing we want for the health of our birds is to have nonnative weed seeds and weeds be out there. The weeds not only hurt habitat biodiversity but the wild birds can fly away and spread the seeds elsewhere."

Recently, Oregon State University researchers discovered up to 14 nonnative weed seed species in bags of seed that were purchased from Corvallis-area stores. The bags included pigweed, Russian thistle, crabgrass, and witchgrass seeds. Each is an invasive weed that's banned by the Oregon Department of Agriculture.

There's more to the problem of bad seed mixes: not only are some seed mixes environmental nuisances by promoting nonnative weeds to grow, but some of the seed mixes that you buy at the store don't even do the job and are a complete waste of your money. Sarah Pinnock is a bird expert at the Jackson Bottom Wetlands Education Center in Hillsboro and told me, "If you see anything on a bag of birdseed that says 'Milo' don't buy it." Pinnock added that many mixes contain a small, dark brown seed, about the size of a BB called Milo that's used as filler: "It's heavy, it's bulky, it fills up the bag and a lot of the birds in this area, frankly, don't eat it." So, it winds up on the ground as waste—and you paid for it too. Best advice: read the label and shop for birdseed as though you're shopping for your family. Instead of buying seed mixes, buy specific environmentally friendly seeds like black oil sunflower seeds. Another tip: Pour enough seed into your filler for only a week (try one-third full to start) because in our wet climate, seed often goes bad before the birds can eat it. You'll help the birds get through winter and help the Northwest outdoors too.

Some bird lovers offer native songbirds shelter in exchange for the sounds of the wild. Hillsboro resident Dennis Frame loves the sights and sounds of the wild, so he builds feeders and houses for native songbirds. Frame's structures aren't really homes, but his elaborate wooden abodes are more akin to, well, bird resorts. Washington County resident Irene Dickson has two of Frame's beautiful yet functional feeders and each is firmly planted in the ground on fence posts 6 feet off the ground in her yard. She said that they "really work." "They add such pleasure and peace," said the avid bird fan. "They're real de-stressers too. Plus, the resort detail is fabulous and impressive with the little rock walls, benches, and other details. It looks like a little cabin by a lake."

Frame is a builder of human homes by trade, but in his cozy and well-organized carpentry shop, he said his greatest pleasure comes from crafting the elaborate bird resorts: "This is my little getaway and I can come in here and get away from it all and get creative too." He's always been a fan of simple, rustic log cabin homes and will often scour the countryside for "models" that he can reproduce on a small scale for the birds: "I'll drive and spot one and 'Oh, that's cool.' Maybe snap a photo or make a mental note and then re-create it in a birdhouse."

Frame has been chippin' away at his hobby for 20 years and said it's the tiny details that impress most people. The resorts sport stone and mortar chimneys, decks with handrails, and small pieces of character that set them apart from ordinary store-bought models—including a wooden front door. He noted, "The door actually opens. I do that because you must clean out the resort following each nesting year. In fact, the birds seldom return the following year unless you do that. I try to make it an easier job."

Frame also trades, barters, and salvages for everything—recycling for the birds. On top of that, he rarely sells a house; instead, through the years he has given them away to nonprofits like his local Rotary Club and the Jackson Bottom Wetlands Education Center. The groups then sell Frame's bird resorts and raise hundreds of dollars to support their educational programs: "This is my way of giving back to the community. I believe in community; they help me out, so I help them out. And getting people out of their houses and learning more about the outdoors is a positive way to go in my book." Many people must agree with Frame. His wildlife work is "red hot" popular and he can't make them fast enough.

You can reach Dennis Frame via e-mail: hackum@comcast.net.

Oregon Birding Trail

*T*here's a new way to explore Oregon and this one is really for the birds. But it's designed for people—especially folks who like to explore destinations where half the fun is in the getting there. The Willamette Valley Birding Trail is a partnership between varied birding groups and Travel Oregon. It offers people a chance to explore more than 130 legitimate birding sites in a region that is home to 70 percent of the state's population. Joel Geier and I recently met at Ankeny National Wildlife Refuge near Albany, Oregon, where he told me that variety is the spice of his birding life along the Willamette Valley Birding Trail: "They're such fascinating creatures; they're feathered, and for me, they have a little more variety than mammals."

Geier knows his birding game well. After all, he's a longtime member of the Oregon Birding Association. His organization participated in creating the Willamette Valley Birding Trail: "We've set it up as twelve different loops in the valley so that if you live in one of the communities in the valley, you can go out on a weekend and visit a loop that includes ten or twelve different sites." It's easy to locate a trail online. A click of your mouse takes you inside one of the dozen different loops where you'll find directions to the sites plus photos of the species that you'll see along the way. "On each of those loops," noted Geier, "there will be sites that you never thought about visiting before and you'll be surprised that they are pretty special places."

Molly Monroe agreed that the Oaks to Wetlands Boardwalk Trail at Ankeny National Wildlife Refuge is one of those special places where you can go birding. "The boardwalk is on pretty level, even terrain and there are benches along that you can rest if you get tired," said Monroe. It's an astonishing wheelchair-accessible trail along 700 feet of elevated boardwalk that leads to an observation blind overlooking a small pond that attracts many different birds. "It is a magnet for wildlife," noted Monroe.

"We'll have thousands upon thousands of ducks and geese and swans here between December and March. We're kind of a little-known secret right now, but I think we're going to become more well-known because there are such excellent wildlife viewing opportunities here and you can get relatively close without disturbing the wildlife."

Not only wintering waterfowl, but also raptor species like bald eagles make the Ankeny National Wildlife Refuge their winter homes. "It's one of the easiest birds for most people to identify so it's fun for them," added Monroe. "Often, you just look out on a tree line of snags and say, 'Oh, there's an eagle perched right there.' Eagles are good because they're well-known by most people and their recovery from near extinction is such a success story." If you're eager to learn more about birding, but you're not sure how to get started, Monroe added that there is good news for the casual first-time visitor.

"Many people come here and don't realize the wealth of birds that they may find on the refuge and so lack some basic tools. We've developed 'family kits' that include everything one would need here. Check out binoculars or a field guide, take it with them out on the hike or drive the auto route, and just bring them back at the end of the day. It's really a great deal." All agree that wildlife viewing along the new Willamette Valley Birding Trail is just the ticket to see Oregon from a different point of view. "Oh, I think it's a huge deal," exclaimed Monroe. "Birding is a growing pastime—and it is one that brings a lot of enjoyment to people of all ages."

36 Ankeny National Wildlife Refuge

Where: 2301 Wintel Road, Jefferson, OR 97352
Web: www.fws.gov/WillametteValley/ankeny
Phone: 503-588-2701

Oregon Birding Trails
Web: www.oregonbirdingtrails.org
Phone: Joel Geier: 541-745-5821

Watch the Episode: www.traveloregon.com/birdingtrail

Winter

Grant McOmie's Outdoor Talk—
A Walk on the Wild and
Woolly Side of Oregon

A few winters ago I found a gem of a get-away that offered one of the deepest perspectives on a wild and woolly chapter of Oregon history. Geologist Rick Thompson had me hooked on an incredible chapter of Oregon's not-so-distant past when he said, "Not many people know this but there was a time when icebergs floated across a gigantic body of water called Lake Allison that stretched the length of the Willamette Valley and it was hundreds of feet deep." Thompson is a detective—not a crime detective but an investigator of Oregon's geologic history and we met during an investigation of several hundred acres of farmland near Gaston, Oregon. He was on the trail of one of the region's oldest mysteries: how hundreds of Montana granite stones ended up in farm fields across the Willamette Valley. "They've been in the ground a very long time," noted Thompson. "Farmers usually plow or till them up and they're often just sitting where the icebergs left them as they melted." Icebergs in Oregon's farm country? "It's true!" said Thompson, a member of the Lower Columbia Chapter of the Ice Age Floods Institute. "The icebergs

just floated around and then reached a certain area and sat there, melted, and these rocks fell out."

Thompson explained that it all came about when ancient, glacial Missoula Lake (in what is now Montana), backed up by an ice dam several miles wide and half a mile high, burst through its western wall and raced across the plains and valleys between Montana and the Pacific Ocean. Thompson said that some 500 cubic miles of floodwater and icebergs "roared across the Northwest, carrying away anything and everything in its path." As the ice flowed, it broke into thousands of pieces, and many of the pieces ended up stranded along the flood route. It may be hard to believe, but it's true! In the blink of a geologic eye, a series of tremendous floods occurred, perhaps twenty times every 50 years for 2,000 years—beginning nearly 14,000 years ago near the end of the Ice Age.

The evidence of icebergs is all around the metro area too; like the hiking trail at Fields Bridge Park along the Tualatin River in West Linn where three granite rocks totaling 46,000 pounds rest along the trail. Thompson's group, the Ice Age Floods Institute, designed the paved, wheelchair-accessible riverside trail complete with several information kiosks along the way. As you stroll you learn much about the remarkable events that occurred 15,000 years ago. In fact, one kiosk offers a colorful map that Thompson created of the Willamette Valley that shows off the ancient Lake Allison, a 400-foot-deep lake that stretched from Kalama, Washington, to Eugene, Oregon.

"I used a topographic map and traced the 400-foot-depth level all the way down to Eugene," said Thompson. "I drew all the nooks and crannies where the valleys would have filled with water and then I went back and put in all the major cities, towns, and highways so people can have a sense and appreciation for how much water there was in the valley." Thompson is a self-proclaimed "flood nut" and said that the huge floods roared through the Columbia River Gorge with water lapping at the ridgetops. He said that the flood events occurred perhaps a hundred times. The floods carried giant granite boulders called erratics deep into the Willamette Valley across Lake Allison. Erratics—a geological term that describes a rock found a considerable distance from its place of origin—range from pebble- to baseball- to car-sized boulders that still dot the Willamette Valley.

Near present-day Sheridan, off Oregon State Highway 18, one giant berg melted and tipped its load, a massive rock that is called the Belleview Boulder. It is the centerpiece of Erratic Rocks State Natural Site and rests on the shoulder of a hillside overlooking the highway. As you hike, notice the gently rolling landscape of the surrounding vineyard-laden hillsides. This landscape is a stark contrast to the Belleview Boulder! Notice the smoothed edges and scratches across the boulder's surface and its sharp angles compared with the rest of the valley. It is a fine place for a picnic lunch and a pause to consider so much dramatic history.

What makes erratics so special? "Oh, the distance from its source," said Thompson. "Plus, it's all granite and to imagine the size of the iceberg that carried a 90-ton rock so far from its source is just amazing." The icebergs floated across Lake Allison for a time and most were pushed west by prevailing winds. When the water dropped and the bergs melted, the granite chunks were left behind—like a ring around the bathtub. "It affected the entire Northwest and shaped the Willamette Valley," said Thompson.

Moreover, the Lake Missoula Floods eventually brought pioneers to Oregon in a roundabout way. It's true! You see, the floods or rock, ice, and other debris scoured the Eastern Washington landscape of all its rich topsoil and then deposited it in the Willamette Valley. It was the same rich topsoil from which early Oregon pioneers built a thriving agricultural economy in the mid-nineteenth century. Thompson speculates, "It's interesting because if the flood and erratic events had not happened, Oregon agriculture might never have developed either."

It is such a powerful and compelling story that nearby Tualatin, Oregon, has embraced it too. In 2010, Yvonne Addington, then president of the Tualatin Historical Society, helped arrange the delivery of two giant erratics that are now displayed at the Tualatin Heritage Center. She said that local folks are betting the erratic story is something people will want to see and know better. Put simply, she believes that "if you display the ancient rocks, people will come."

"We have a strong interest in the Ice Age here," said Addington. "A local man discovered a woolly mammoth skeleton in 1962 [it is displayed in the Tualatin City Library] and that has led into erratics conveying the power of nature that shaped our community. It's something that visitors and residents can enjoy and it has a special quality that no other city really offers."

Back out in Washington County, Thompson continued to track down more erratics across farmland as he develops a new "Ice Age Trail." He wants travelers to someday journey across the region and learn more about the powerful forces that shaped the Oregon we know today. "It's a detective story," he said. "And I love mysteries!"

January

37

A Convocation of Eagles

I must admit that I feel rather confident about my identification knowledge of Oregon's varied wildlife species and yet when it comes to the names we give "collections" of wildlife I am often stumped. The plurality of a species sends shivers down my spine. Did you know that many deer are called a herd, but they can also be called a bevy? A collection of elk is not a herd but a gang? Collections of birds can be called flocks or flights, but geese can also be called a gaggle or a skein. And that brings us to our nation's symbol: bald eagles never gather in flocks but something far more regal called a convocation.

You can find this wildlife moment atop 4-story-tall cottonwoods near Tangent, Oregon, where a convocation draws up to 100 eagles in the Linn County treetops each evening. Even more remarkable, according to Jeff Fleischer, a retired US Fish and Wildlife Refuge manager, is that this convocation of eagles didn't exist 5 years ago. Fleischer has tallied a rapid rise in the wintertime Willamette Valley eagle population: "We have seen a wholesale increase, a doubling and then tripling of bald eagles in the southern end of the Willamette Valley."

Fleischer is a member of the East Cascades Audubon Society and he leads a statewide Raptor Survey Project; he will drive more than 2,400 miles across Willamette Valley main lines and back roads to count eagles in trees, on poles, in fields, or in flight. Over the last several years, a typical high count for a winter's day was fifty. Fleischer said that in 2013 the number "skyrocketed."

"We had 217 in one day!" Fleischer said he thinks more eagles have arrived in the Willamette Valley because the dining is so good: "During the winter, a lot of sheep will die for various reasons and the carcasses are left in the fields. That's what eagles key on without question." Fleischer said the winter sheep population has grown because farmers have changed the types of grass they grow for

Oregon's grass seed market. New grasses tolerate winter grazing and allow farmers to make more money by grazing more flocks of sheep. "The increase in sheep brought the increase in eagles," noted Fleischer. "It's an easily accessed food source and eagles don't have to expend a lot of energy to eat."

Joel Geier, a member of the Oregon Birding Association, described eagle viewing opportunities: "You may see eagles standing on the ground, perched in trees, or flying across the fields—they are distinct and hard to miss." Geier said visitors can follow the Santiam Loop of the Willamette Valley Birding Trail that goes past the eagle convocation in Linn County: "You don't need fancy optics to see eagles because they are so big. Some may be seen just a hundred yards off the roadway."

Steve Seibel photographs eagles and has documented their feeding behavior: "Typically, the birds displace each other—that is, one will feed for a while and then another will come in and move the first bird away. The food seems to be so abundant that they don't fight to hold their position." Geier reminds visitors that etiquette demands you pull to the side of the road and not block private roads or driveways: "Be aware that almost everything 10 feet off the road is private land," said Geier. "So stay on the shoulder of the roadway and don't wander across fields."

You can observe eagles in the Willamette Valley. Molly Monroe, US Fish and Wildlife Biologist at William L. Finley National Wildlife Refuge near Corvallis, said that there are three national wildlife refuges—William L. Finley, Ankeny, and Baskett Slough—that are easily accessed public settings to see bald eagles and thousands of waterfowl: "As long as you find open bodies of water where there are ducks and geese, it's a given you'll see one or two eagles. They are always on watch, either perched or actively hunting." For information about Oregon's birding trails and to get the weekly wildlife report about birds and other wildlife activity, visit the Oregon Department of Fish and Wildlife bird-watching page.

37A Santiam Loop, Tangent and vicinity
Where: Along US Highway 99E, 5 miles south of Albany
Web: www.oregonbirdingtrails.org/willamettevalley.htm
Phone: Joel Geier: 541-745-5821

37B Baskett Slough National Wildlife Refuge
Where: 10995 State Highway 22, Dallas, OR 97338
Web: www.fws.gov/refuge/baskett_slough
Phone: 503-623-2749

Watch the Episode: www.traveloregon.com/eagleconvocation

Back from the Brink

oday, you can see bald eagles in every region of the state: soaring along coastal headlands like Cape Meares State Scenic Viewpoint; perched in the cottonwoods above industrial Portland's Smith and Bybee Wetlands Natural Area, or across the open fields of the greater Willamette Valley; and eagles are frequently seen throughout the entire Columbia River basin. Bald eagles are kings of the sky once more! At the Jackson Bottom Wetlands Preserve, a pair of eagles has built a massive nest that's proven productive over the past 3 years and they've raised eaglets each season. In fact, the nest is the third in the past 14 years (the others blew down in severe storms). Sarah Pinnock, Jackson Bottom Wetlands Preserve education specialist, said that biologists estimate the pair has raised a dozen youngsters. Eagles build their nests on the tops of tall trees or on cliffs. Nests can be 6 feet across and 6 to 8 feet high. A pair of eagles will use the same nest year after year. Typically, the female lays two eggs that

Bald eagles have returned from the brink of extinction in Oregon and are now found in every corner of the state.

hatch after about 35 days. Fledging may take as long as 12 weeks, and parents may care for their young for about 4 to 6 weeks after fledging. Fish are a major component of the bald eagle's diet, but bald eagles will eat a variety of animals and carrion, including waterfowl and small mammals.

Inside the nearby Jackson Bottom Wetlands Education Center, you get a close-up look at amazing eagle architecture in an actual nest. The nest was rescued from a giant cottonwood that had been damaged in a windstorm and was falling over. The nest was cut, removed, and transported intact to the center so to teach us more about eagles. "The first thing people remark on is the size of the nest; it's huge," said Pinnock. "From a distance, an eagle nest appears like a dark spot in a tree but here you get up close to this one. It seems about the size of a Mini Cooper or a Beetle car. It's really impressive."

Pinnock added that each year, the eagle parents will add up to 2 feet of new material to the nest. The birds work together and they weave sticks and branches into the existing nest with their beaks and talons. "They line the top of the nest with soft material like grasses or small debris," said Pinnock. "They create a comfortable, cup-shaped depression in the nest and that's where the female will lay her eggs." The female eagle will lay up to three eggs each March and the eggs usually hatch within a month. The chicks will fledge from the nest in about 8 weeks. Young eagles stay with their parents through July and then the entire family disappears. The parents return to the nest site again in November. Pinnock said the recovery of bald eagles in Oregon is a remarkable event: "Twenty years ago, I remember rarely seeing a bald eagle—except perhaps the coast—and now we have several pair nesting in the Tualatin River basin alone. The eagles are back in big numbers and I think that's just fabulous news."

37C (4A on the map) Jackson Bottom Wetlands

Where: 2600 SW Hillsboro Highway, Hillsboro, OR 97123

Web: www.jacksonbottom.org

Phone: 503-681-6206

Watch the Episode: www.traveloregon.com/backfromthebrink

38

The B-52s of the Waterfowl World

*T*housands of visitors travel to Oregon during the winter months, but one particular group of guests sports a unique nickname that sets them apart: the B-52s of the waterfowl world. Tundra swans are huge, easy to admire, and you can spot them at a favorite pond, wetland, or wildlife area each winter. I always enjoy the unexpected treats that come when waterfowl put on quite a show. "Waterfowl are distinct, colorful, and just the most in-your-face animals that are around us . . . and the number you can see is just so much higher than other wildlife," according to Metro naturalist James Davis.

Davis and I met at the popular Coon Point Overlook of Sturgeon Lake at the Sauvie Island Wildlife Area. The 12,000-acre state refuge can be a fine place to admire waterfowl from a distance. That's especially true for tundra swans, the long-distance travelers of the waterfowl world. Few wildlife come close to surpassing the tundra swan's remarkable journey: some birds make a 10,000-mile round-trip migration from the Arctic to Mexico wintering grounds and then back home again. "Well, for one, they are huge," said Davis. "Swans are among the biggest flying and heaviest birds in the world. That's just spectacular to me and then they're pure white and that is great."

Another prime spot to observe tundra swans is Trojan Pond near Rainier, Oregon. The route between Portland and Astoria may not be the fastest, but that's all right with me because I can pull off and watch the B-52s of the waterfowl world. The pond and adjacent nature park is owned by Portland General Electric and is open to visitors seasonally. The pull-off at the pond is open anytime. It's where flocks of tundra swans seem to fill the sky on 6-foot wingspans and then glide in for a well-deserved break. Tundra swans have wintered at this pond for decades and their stark white feathers are an impressive contrast against the

Each year, tundra swans make a 4,000-mile round-trip journey from the Arctic to Oregon.

otherwise drab backdrop of water and surrounding forest. The big birds really do light up the scene. Swans mate for life and each winter they fly from sub-Arctic homes to arrive in Oregon with their families—including young-of-the-year birds called cygnets that are mottled in black and gray feathers as though covered in soot. At a distance, they look like so many cotton balls, silent and majestic, floating atop the water. Davis was quick to note that their serene appearance is deceiving, for under the water it is all action—to survive: "Swans don't dive under the water like many ducks do to get food. They tip over and stretch their long necks down [over 2 feet long] to reach any kind of plant material that may be growing in a pond or lake."

The big birds winter across the entire state too. Fernhill Wetlands in Washington County is an excellent hideout to catch a view of tundra swans. So is Baskett Slough National Wildlife Refuge in Polk County where the visitor access is just off State Highway 22, west of Salem. Further afield, try the Klamath Marsh National Wildlife Area in Southern Oregon where the swan show is reliable all winter long until the big birds head back to the Arctic in March.

At the Sauvie Island Wildlife Area, up to 2,000 swans winter across the 12,000-acre site. Wildlife Area Assistant Manager Mathew Keenan noted that the state wildlife area is a fine host for up to 200,000 waterfowl: "We do attract a lot of wildlife because we're such a large target for them as they pass through. We have large tracts of protected areas without development and that's the big advantage. We manage for waterfowl here, so in addition to natural wetlands we plant food crops specifically for the wildlife." Keenan added that the popular wildlife area caters to visitors—both those with feathers and those without: "We have three primary locations this time of year: One is Coon Point Overlook to Sturgeon Lake where you can always see waterfowl. Another is further down Reeder Road to our Wildlife Viewing Platform. And finally, visitors can drive down Rentenaar Road. Folks can travel up and down that road and get a good look at varied wetland habitat types. They are allowed out of their vehicles as long as they stay on the road, but they cannot go walking through the marshes."

Wildlife books can be lifesavers for the beginning waterfowl watcher and Davis has written a dandy called *The Northwest Nature Guide: Where to Go and What to See*. The book's many color photos make wildlife identification easy. "It's all about nature," noted Davis. "Plants, all kinds of animals, plus I included destinations—important things to see. It's also organized month to month, so you can see things any time of year." And seeing things clearly is important too. Davis added that you should include binoculars or a spotting scope with your wildlife-watching gear. "Swans are not hard to spot," said Davis, "but many smaller duck species can be difficult to identify from a long distance, so I never leave home without my scope and my binoculars. Both make a big difference." Also, remember that waterfowl hunting is a part of the Sauvie Island Wildlife Area management scene through January. You can check the Oregon Department of Fish and Wildlife website to determine a hunt day and plan your wildlife watching trips on nonhunting days. And be sure you purchase an Oregon State Wildlife Area Parking Permit. It is required if you leave your vehicle for any time.

38A (30 on the map) Sauvie Island Wildlife Area

Where: 18330 NW Sauvie Island Road, Portland, OR 97231

Web: www.dfw.state.or.us

Phone: 503-621-3488

38B Coon Point Overlook

Where: Located near Milepost 3 on Reeder Road

Web: www.dfw.state.or.us

Phone: 503-621-3488

Watch the Episode: www.traveloregon.com/tundraswans

39

Cascades Raptor Center

*I*f you're a fan of Oregon wildlife, winter is the best season to catch the sky show of waterfowl and raptors that migrate through the state. There's goose "song" in the air—have you heard the excited sound? It's hard to miss as the flocks seem to shout: "We're here! In Oregon at last!" Fast on the tail feathers of the abundant waterfowl flocks are the raptors: the hundreds of hawks and eagles that pass through or winter over in Oregon.

You'll want to stop in and winter awhile at the Cascades Raptor Center near Eugene. It's a wildlife rehabilitation clinic that helps the sick and injured birds of prey. Scores of birds, like a red-tailed hawk, a barn owl, a white-tailed kite, arrive at the center each winter thanks to well-intentioned folks who often recover the hurt birds in the field. "I wanted to create a nature center that helped raptors," said the center's director, Louise Shimmel. "My goal for the past 30 years has been to have representatives from each Northwest species of raptors for the public to see and learn from and now we're very close to that goal." In fact, the Cascades Raptor Center has been in operation since 1990 as a wildlife hospital and education site. You can see and learn about thirty-four different raptor species across the 3-acre site. Shimmel said that education about raptors has made a big difference to our understanding and appreciation of the birds: "Absolutely! Raptors have had a huge perception shift from vermin and bounties to majestic and beautiful. Back in the 1950s, there were bounties on hawks and eagles and today we understand the value of the predator-prey cycle."

Still, thoughtless injuries persist. Shimmel showed off a Swainson's hawk that was shot by a poacher. Its pelvis shattered, the young raptor will never fly again. So it has become an ambassador of sorts, in schools and at the center, teaching people more about raptors. Volunteer Dan Gleason said that the Cascades

"Handler talks" are a daily feature that teaches visitors more about raptors like this peregrine falcon.

Raptor Center is a fine place to visit and learn what the varied raptors look like before heading out to see them in the wild: "That's one way—you can see them up close and then go out and see them in their natural habitat. That helps folks understand what they see." Gleason added that bald eagles are a favorite for many birders because the big birds are more common, even abundant, in some parts of Oregon and because they are easy to spot, especially sporting the tell-tale white head and tail feathers that mark a mature bald eagle. "We have reached a point in the Willamette Valley, particularly throughout Lane County, where people see bald eagles more often than other raptor species. We really get a big influx of the birds moving through here each winter."

The Cascades Raptor Center is also a perfect place to begin your raptor watching adventures. The center offers "handler talks" each Saturday and Sunday at 1:00 P.M. sharp. It's a great chance to get a close-up view of many raptor species and the handler will teach you much about the species too. You can also find additional places to watch for waterfowl and raptors at the new ODFW Wildlife Viewing Map. It's a fine resource for locating the best wildlife viewing sites across Oregon.

39 Cascades Raptor Center

Where: 32275 Fox Hollow Road, Eugene, OR 97405

Web: www.eraptors.org

Phone: 541-485-1320

Watch the Episode: www.traveloregon.com/raptorcenter

40

A Bull Elk Romance

*N*ot long ago, one of the luckiest wildlife encounters occurred right in a small Eastern Oregon town and left a lasting impression that will be the talk of that town for years. In "The Valley of Peace" at La Grande, Oregon, in the shadow of the Blue Mountains, a very lonely Rocky Mountain bull elk went looking for love and found himself stranded in a sea of human hubbub. The story started in a suburb of this small Union County burg, on a crisp, cool, and brilliant September morning. Local resident Jim Brown was going about his weekly chore of cleaning the leaves from his yard. He had yard work, not wildlife, on his mind, until his

neighbor urgently called him aside and whispered that he'd better take a gander into the side yard, where Brown had a number of guests.

"I put the ladder down and went over," he explained to me, "and there—in the middle of my yard—is the biggest bull elk I have ever seen, just lying down back there. Talk about amazed. Good Lord! It was something." It was something all right. Nine hundred pounds of some-thing that sported a towering set of sharp antlers, six points to a side. The elk was huge and awesome and resting on Brown's green grass. But how, you may wonder, did a back-

Rocky Mountain bull elk sport impressive antlers and the animals can tip the scales at 800 pounds.

Daily feeding keeps the elk herds on the Elkhorn Wildlife Area rather than nearby farmlands.

woods critter end up smack in the middle of La Grande? Jim Cadwell, a local wildlife biologist, told me that the bull's behavior had a simple explanation–the elk had love on his mind: "La Grande sits on the doorstep of the magnificent Blue Mountains, and we have cow [female] elk coming into the outskirts of town all the time. Since September is the peak of the rut or breeding season, there's a good possibility that this male was looking for a mate."

Yes, it seems the bull elk was looking for love; and he ran past the local Safeway grocery store, cruised through downtown along Main Street, zipped by the Elks Lodge without hesitation, and then made a sharp turn onto Second Avenue to find it. His route to romance picked up quite a gawking crowd too. Three miles and 20 minutes later, the poor boy was nearly exhausted and practically collapsed in Jim Brown's side yard. Word spread among the locals like wildfire, and soon nearly a hundred people were watching from a short distance. The police had their hands full controlling the swelling crowd, who sported cameras and binoculars amid a carnival-like atmosphere.

According to Stan Terry, formerly of the Oregon State Police, love had put this bull and the police in a pickle. He explained, "I was really afraid that somebody might get gored, because the elk was really agitated. He'd snap his teeth, scratch the ground with his hooves, and he was definitely aggressive. We didn't have a lot of answers about what to do next either." For nearly 2 hours, folks wrestled with ideas and ways to move him out of town. Some said they could rope the bull, others thought to drug him with a tranquilizing dart, and a handful suggested they could solve the dilemma with their hunting rifles. All these ideas were ruled out due to safety concerns, but the police were nervous because time was running out. The poor beast might collapse from the trauma of it all.

That's when Brian Chamberlain stepped forward with a better plan: He'd call the big bull out of town. Chamberlain, an accomplished hunter, had a simple idea to give the big boy what he wanted. Chamberlain was adept at using a special cow call that, with practice, emits the not-so-sultry sounds of a female elk looking for a mate. The cry is somewhat akin to a high-pitched squeal from an out-of-kilter, floppy fan belt. But if it's presented correctly, the sound is an offer that bull elk cannot refuse. Chamberlain moved up the street a block or two and gave two short whistles. Stan Terry described what happened next: "It was the darndest thing. That bull perked up his tall ears and swiveled them around like radar dishes. He listened, then his head snapped to the left and his eyes got big as saucers. I swear he smacked his lips before he shot off like cannon fire in Chamberlain's direction. That bull elk was on a dead run, and he had lust on his mind."

Chamberlain suddenly realized he'd better move or he'd soon have a lap full of elk: "Stan yelled at me, 'Start running now, Brian!' I looked around the corner and thought, Oh, my gosh! He's headed right at me. His nose was up in the air and he was looking all around." I quickly asked, "Looking for love?" Chamberlain laughed nervously and said, "Oh, yeah, probably, but not from me. That's why I wanted to keep ahead of him. So I started running too. I had to run faster and faster to stay ahead of the elk because he was just picking up his feet and putting them down faster and faster too." For block after block, that's how it went down, as Chamberlain, the elk "Pied Piper," called, then ran, then led a romantic elk up and down streets for miles.

Finally, they reached the forested foothills, and thankfully, the elk was home free. "It must have been pretty funny for folks to gape up the street and see this bull chasing after me," Chamberlain chuckled. He hinted at a certain pride for having saved the day and saved a majestic elk from certain death. Stan Terry was very thankful no one was hurt and said the tale of "La Grande's Romantic Elk" is destined to become legend: "Yeah, it's one for the memory banks for sure—the day a lonely bull elk went looking for love and became the biggest show in our town."

You won't need to chase elk or be chased by them to enjoy one of the finest winter elk view sites in Eastern Oregon at the Elkhorn Wildlife Area near Baker City. From mid-November through February, you can see as many as 150 Rocky Mountain elk. A deer and elk feeding program has been in place for many years at the 10,000-acre refuge so that the animals will not venture into the Baker Valley and damage farmers' haystacks. According to the area's manager, Ed Miguez, it's a program that's worked very well: "Preventing crop damage was the reason the state created the wildlife area in the early 1970s, and it's why we've added acreage and feed sites several times since." The state's solution has been a success, too, as the problem of elk and deer marauding haystacks is only a memory for most landowners in the Baker, Bowen, and North Powder Valleys.

You are encouraged to bring a camera and bundle up against the chilly 15 degrees; expect a dusting of snow falling too. On our visit, we witnessed interesting behaviors of young male elk sparring with one another—testing each other's strength with their antlers. We learned that elk and deer are not the only wildlife here, for predators are often seen flanking the herd. In fact, we quickly spotted a coyote in the nearby tree line intently watching the herd. It's not unusual to see several coyote, even an occasional cougar, checking out the herd. You can learn a lot about predator-prey relationships as nature's often dramatic struggle between life and death is played out here all winter.

---

40 Elkhorn Wildlife Area

Where: 61846 Powder River Lane, North Powder, OR 97867
Web: www.dfw.state.or.us
Phone: 541-898-2826

Winter Truffles

The best adventures are the ones that entice and intrigue you down the trail—the ones that promise yet unseen rewards, perhaps a treasure for your efforts. That was the assurance from new friends who invited me to join their different sort of "field hunt" in the lush Willamette Valley. The recent hunt relied on a keen canine sense of smell and willingness to dig in the duff to find valuable Oregon truffles. Kris Jacobson is a professional dog trainer who operates a business called Umami Truffle Dogs. Her partner is Ilsa, a 5-year-old Belgian Malinois breed of dog prized for its nose. "The nose knows," said Jacobson when I joined her team near Eugene in a Lane County forest. The two hunt together in dark stands of 30-year-old Doug fir and their hunting success depends on Ilsa's famous nose.

The prizes they seek are gorgeous, walnut-sized fungi that are more famous than you'd think. You see, Oregon truffles are blessed with aromatic, almost pungent, scents that are culinary treasures. In fact, Jacobson said that the truffle's strong aroma makes the finding easy for a trained dog like Ilsa. "I give her a search command and she ventures out ahead of me," noted Jacobson. "I pretty much stay put and keep an eye on her as she wanders about me trying to pick up the scent of the truffle." It didn't take Ilsa long to find a truffle treasure. She dipped her head, sniffed the ground, scratched the surface twice, and shook her head to signal a find. "Ilsa tends to stop right on top of them," said Jacobson. "She might nick it a little bit with her paw but by and large she'll stop at the top of it." Jacobson said that her job is to keep watch and follow Ilsa's signs: "There's one right close to the surface—right there—and it's a big one."

Oregon's white truffles vary from acorn- to walnut-sized and offer a savory—even pungent—taste to food.

Ten years ago, Jacobson knew virtually nothing about truffles—what she calls a "mushroom that grows underground." That changed when she tasted her first wild Oregon white truffle. "A nice, ripe truffle should have a distinct vein running through it, almost like marbling through a high quality steak. It's got this amazing aroma coming out of it; a strong garlic-cheese-like aroma. It's very savory, and it makes you hungry."

Between 2 and 10 tons of Oregon truffles are harvested from Doug fir forests each year. The harvest varies annually depending upon climate and weather patterns during a season that stretches between November and February. Oregon chef Karl Zenk of Marché restaurant in Eugene said truffles have a remarkable ability to transform meals from delicious to out of this world: "You've got the earthiness of the meat and the vegetables, and the truffle kind of accentuates that and gives it a nice roundness of flavor and aroma that's just special. Truffles are something we can really celebrate in Oregon. We are proud of them—such a great thing."

Back in the forest, Oregon truffle expert and mycologist Dr. Charles Lefevre said Oregon truffles are world-class delicacies but not known widely. The so-called underground mushroom ranges in size from a pea to a grapefruit and it is unrivaled in the kitchen. It grows throughout western Oregon. "Habitat is typically farmland that has been converted to Douglas fir," said Lefevre. "It's often a crop found right in people's backyards, orchards, or forest stands."

Jacobson added that truffle hunting is a lot of fun because she can spend a day in the field with her best friend and come home with a delicious reward. "Just being outdoors with Ilsa and watching her work is fun. Both of us enjoy each other's company and accomplishing a task together." You can learn more about truffles at the annual Oregon Truffle Festival that is held the last weekend each January. You can pick up tips, techniques, and sample recipes at the fabulous affair that's held in Eugene. If you want to learn more about Oregon truffles, visit natruffling.org (North American Truffling Society, based in Corvallis).

Umami Truffle Dogs
Web: umamitruffledogs.com
Phone: 541-632-4105
Watch the Episode: www.traveloregon.com/trufflehunt

41

Eagle Watch

*I*f you love Oregon's wide-open vistas, consider weekend travel to Central Oregon's Lake Billy Chinook where newcomers and experienced birders enjoy spectacular views of birds of prey during the annual Eagle Watch cosponsored by Portland General Electric (PGE) and Oregon State Parks. The event is held annually at PGE's Round Butte Overlook Park; a good place to duck in to learn more about Lake Billy Chinook (the lake formed when Round Butte Dam was completed in 1964) plus the eagles and other wildlife that live in the area. It is the main site for the Eagle Watch event that draws folks from all over the west during the last full weekend in February. Oregon State Parks Interpretive Ranger Paul Patton noted that many people come to Eagle Watch to learn more from the eagle experts and guest speakers who attend the two-day event. "Eagle Watch has grown into a major event for our region," said Patton. "You can learn about the natural and cultural history of this area and usually see plenty of eagles. It is great fun for the entire family and it's free. Whether you're a firs-time eagle viewer or seasoned researcher, Eagle Watch offers something for everybody."

Framed by towering 400-foot canyon walls, Lake Billy Chinook offers a unique perspective on Central Oregon that also provides plenty of elbow room. The lake,

Bald eagles soar on thermals above the sheer rock cliffs of Lake Billy Chinook in Central Oregon.

The Deschutes, Crooked, and Metolius Rivers join to create the 7-mile-long Lake Billy Chinook.

due west of Madras, is framed by the snow-covered Cascade Mountains to the west and a vast undulating high desert to the east. It is big country where distances are great and people are few. But Patton said that when it comes to Eagle Watch, the lack of people is actually a good thing: "There are some days when you will see more bald eagles and golden eagles than you do people in the park. It's just stunning to watch the wildlife."

He's right. We found a compelling wildlife show at Cove Palisades State Park's Viewpoint Number 2. The spacious viewpoint offers a breathtaking view of the lake and its varied canyons, but we were soon drawn to a more dramatic life and death show that played out hundreds of feet below us on the lake's surface.

Not one, but two, bald eagles repeatedly buzzed a flock of ducks. The little waterfowl were bunched up, wing to wing, so to avoid getting caught by the eagle's sharp talons. We watched this age-old predator-prey game marked by multiple eagle dives, with talons extended, for more than 15 minutes. It was a remarkable activity amid a timeless rimrock country on a lake that's more than 7 miles long.

Don't forget binoculars for they make a big difference in enjoying the view of bald eagles.

PGE Wildlife Biologist Robert Marheine said that Lake Billy Chinook has been a drawing card for the eagles for many years: "Well, it's a combination of plentiful food [the lake is home to bountiful kokanee salmon] plus huge, rocky cliff escarpments that provide preferred raptor roosting and nesting habitat—it's a special place." Marheine was quick to add that wintertime eagle viewing demands preparation including warm clothing, powerful but comfortable binoculars, and finally, lots of patience. "I don't know how many times we've been out here with people who say, 'Ahh, I don't see an eagle,' said Marheine, "and they jump into their cars and leave. Too bad! Usually, that's when a bald eagle comes right up to us on a thermal and drifts over our heads. If you bring patience, you will be rewarded."

41 (11C on the map) Cove Palisades State Park

Where: 7300 Jordan Road, Culver, OR 97734

Web: www.oregonstateparks.org

Phone: 541-546-3412 or 800-551-6949

Watch the Episode: www.traveloregon.com/eaglewatch

42

Lend a Hand at
Jewell Meadows

ou'll want to bundle up against the cold when you go aboard the Jewell Meadows Wildlife Area hay wagon to feed the herd of Roosevelt elk. On a recent February daybreak, cold and crisp and quiet conditions greeted the visitor across the 700-acre Jewell Meadows (this is one part of the expansive Jewell Meadows Wildlife Area). Despite the mercury holding steady at just 7 degrees, the otherwise silent morning came to life when the hay wagon came into view and 200 elk quickly responded.

Prized for their size and impressive antlers, Roosevelt elk at Jewell Wildlife Area are easy to spy from several lookouts.

Wildlife Area Manager Bryan Swearingen said the morning feeding is a regular winter event across Jewell Meadows—the feeding keeps the elk on the wildlife area rather than foraging across nearby private agricultural lands. "OK, folks," whispered Swearingen, "this hay comes off in little flakes and if we could drop a flake off every 10 feet or so that would be perfect. The tractor will tow the wagon slowly across the field and we'll feed two bales of the hay to the elk this morning."

We were on the western fringe of the refuge, an area where approximately twenty-five bull elk spend their time together. Swearingen noted that this group is referred to as the "bachelor herd": "The bulls use so much energy during the breeding season from September through early October that they can go into winter in real poor condition. So, they're trying to regain that

Don't be late for a ride on the daily hay wagon for it leaves the parking area each morning at 8 o'clock sharp.

energy and fat reserves to make it through the wintertime." Some of the bulls in the Jewell herd are massive animals that tip the scales at more than 800 pounds with antler spans of 5 or even 6 feet. On this particular day, there was another sound on board the feeding wagon as Dean Crouser's camera made the telltale click-click-click of auto mode as he snapped shots with his digital camera that had a 200mm zoom lens attached to it.

Crouser sported a mile-wide smile on his face and beamed, "I'm a native Oregonian and I've always been proud to be an Oregonian. This is one more thing that makes it such a cool place to be. This is just another little gem." Crouser is a wildlife artist who searches for Oregon wildlife in everyday moments—the times that many of us take for granted. This day marked his first wintertime trip to Jewell Meadows Wildlife Area and he was a bit like a kid in a candy store. So many photo opportunities were presented in front of him from the cozy confines of the feeding wagon because the elk were feeding just 20 yards away. "I am looking for just the right light," he noted. "The contrast of the dark and the light with a bull's head turned to where it's in the shadow; a real dark tone but his back is all lit up and a nice yellowish orange. Like that one right there."

It's what has long stirred Crouser's imagination: "It really is the stuff that I've seen and done nearly all my life in the Northwest. Elk are kind of the cherry on top of our big game animals in Oregon. Yet, across the country there aren't a lot of places that have them. They're pretty special." Crouser travels across Oregon, often corner to corner, and his work reflects the adventure and inspiration and wild moments that he has seen. While his work begins with a camera (on this day he will take more than 400 photos, but only a handful will be used as reference models), all too soon paintbrushes and watercolors take over in his Gresham, Oregon, studio: "I do not strive to replicate the animals. It doesn't have to be accurate from the standpoint of what an elk really looks like. Now a lot of people really like to paint that way, almost photo-realism. I appreciate people who can, but I have no interest in doing that."

Crouser has had many interests in his life and he has set many records too. Like the NCAA Track and Field Championships that he won back in the early '80s at the University of Oregon. A few years ago he was inducted into the University's Hall of Fame. In addition to his athletic successes, he said that he's been painting since he was 10 years old. It has grown into a passion for his home state that he likes to share with others: "Elk and deer are obviously intelligent animals and it's pretty neat to watch their mannerisms and feeding activities and then, especially with elk, how the bulls and younger bulls determine their hierarchy. That's what makes Jewell pretty cool. Anyone would love to go out and see it—even for an hour. How could you not? It's incredible."

42 (11B on the map) Jewell Meadows Wildlife Area

Where: 79878 State Highway 202, Seaside, OR 97138

Web: www.dfw.state.or.us

Phone: 503-755-2264

Watch the Episode: www.traveloregon.com/jewellwildlife

Mussels for the Taking

*Y*ears ago on a rare, windless February afternoon, I met Dale Snow, then a retired fishery biologist with the Oregon Department of Fish and Wildlife, at Seal Rock State Wayside. The wayside is a state park and interpretive site with trails and information kiosks that teach about Oregon's intertidal zone. It boasts many large offshore rocks, inhabited by seals, sea lions, seabirds, and other marine life. The wayside includes interesting tide pools, as well as excellent ocean views and a sandy beach. Developed for day use, the picnic area occupies a pleasant stand of shore pine, spruce, and salal.

We had timed our visit just prior to the ebb tide, so the rocks were fully exposed and Snow estimated we had two solid hours to use our muscles to gather our mussels. As we walked along the sand toward a promising car-sized boulder whose top half was roofed with mussels and barnacles, Snow remarked, "When the tide goes out, my dinner table is set." Then he explained the need for that weed puller I'd purchased the night before: "This is nothing more than a dandelion puller for your garden, but I like to use it for mussel pulling too." With that, he gently probed a small cluster of 4-inch mussels down to where they were attached to the rock.

Mussels attach themselves to rocks and each other with thin but incredibly strong stringlike threads called bissel. They grow these threads like a man might grow a beard. Like oysters and

Clusters of mussels are held in place by stringlike threads called bissel.

Steamed Mussels

Snow's recipe proved as simple as it was delightful to eat: Combine a half cup of white wine and a cup of water. Bring the liquid to a boil in a steamer pot, then add 24 mussels and steam them for about 20 minutes (until they've opened completely). Don't overcook the mussels as they lose their flavor and become tough as leather, as does all shellfish. Dip in warm garlic butter.

clams, mussels are bivalve filter feeders that siphon nutrients from the sea as the ocean rises to cover them. Unlike oysters and clams, mussels take a beating from the relentless pounding of the surf, so the little creatures hold on for their very lives with their bissel threads.

"Bissel with gristle," I joked to Snow as I admired the iridescent blue-pearl overlay on the otherwise drab, brown shell. Snow explained that the nutritional value of mussels has been recognized for countless generations. "There are many rocky areas along the coastal shore where you'll find mussels," he said, "and it's interesting to visit Indian middens [mounds marking former Native American encampments]. They are often filled with mussel shells, as well as clams and oysters. They knew a good thing when they found it."

Quarter-sized barnacles encrusted the 4-inch mussels, and we simply knocked them off with our handy tools. Within minutes I was ready for part two of Snow's beach-stop lesson. Oregon requires you purchase a shellfish license before you gather up to seventy-two mussels per person. We took only what we were prepared to eat that afternoon—about a dozen each.

We feasted on fresh steamed mussels dipped in warm garlic butter and could only imagine what we might have paid to enjoy this fine gastronomic treat at a restaurant. As we admired the remarkable rock formations disappearing under the fast-rising tide, the winter sun winked across the sheltered tide pools. Snow confided that mussel collecting was but a part of the wintertime coastal scene he's long enjoyed. "Winter's just an excellent time. You don't have hordes of people here. A lot of folks just go roaring by from city to city and bypass the beaches. I guess they think the only time to go for a walk along the sand is summertime. Oh sure, it can be a bit chilly, but I really think we see more sun in the wintertime than we ever do in the summer."

43 Seal Rock State Wayside

Where: About 10 miles south of Newport, OR

Web: www.dfw.state.or.us

Phone: 541-867-4741

If You Go—Shellfish Safety

The Oregon Division of Health is responsible for monitoring shellfish safety for recreational clamming and mussel collection. Red tide, or paralytic shellfish poisoning (PSP), is a serious concern along Oregon and Washington beaches. It is caused by eating shellfish contaminated with algae that contains a toxin harmful to humans. When this algae increases to high numbers in marine waters, the condition is commonly referred to as a red tide. The poison is not destroyed by cooking or freezing. The amount of toxin increases when water conditions are favorable. However, the exact combination of conditions that causes blooms of poison-producing plankton is not known. The Northwest Fisheries Science Center's (NWFSC) Marine Biotoxin Program provides information and services to the public.

Shellfish Safety Hotline Food Safety: 800-448-2474

Columbia River Smelt

hey call it a run, but that's not really true. Packed fin to fin, the small fish, called smelt, glide and swim in the clear, shallow river water. You can easily see them by three, four, and scores galore. But wait! The fact is, as measured by the commercial fishing nets stuffed with thousands and thousands more, it's not a run at all. Each February, you could say there's a stampede of the tiny fish up the Columbia River and then the runs branch out into tributaries like Washington's Cowlitz River and Oregon's Sandy River. It's an annual event for dedicated anglers who could care less about cold, bone-chilling winter water. Some fishing folk, clad in neoprene rubber waders, will stand waist deep or even higher just to find the right spot. Then, armed with telescopic-handled dip nets, the anglers reach far out, drop their nets into the icy river, and, with a downstream sweep, attempt to snare as many of the prized, silvery, wriggly, squirmy masses of smelt as possible.

Steve King, retired fishery biologist for the Oregon Department of Fish and Wildlife, told me that "smelt" or "hooligans" are eulachon (pronounced YU-la-kon), the Native American name for the Columbia River smelt, known in scientific circles as *Thaleichthys pacificus*. Smelts are small, not reaching more than a foot in length and, like Pacific salmon, the smelt are anadromous, spawning in freshwater but migrating to the ocean to feed and grow. The tiny fish swim in large schools and begin a spawning migration at age three or four. They typically enter the Columbia River in early to mid-January, finding tributaries in mid- to late January. The females deposit their eggs over a sandy river bottom, and the eggs attach to the sand and silt. After hatching, the tiny fry move out to the ocean to feed and grow.

When the smelt run up the Sandy River near Troutdale, Oregon, so do thousands of people and you'd think you'd arrived at the "Smelt Capital of Oregon." People perch on shoreline rocks or wade in the river to dip and catch pounds of the fish. Smelt are a high-protein fish that, in addition to being pan-fried or smoked for human consumption, are widely used as fish food at aquariums and marine parks. Smelt dipping is a Pacific Northwest pastime, and you'll often see young kids, their parents, and their grandparents making an afternoon adventure of the event. It is great outdoor fun and, some say, hints of warmer spring days to come. Smelt dipping nets can be purchased in area sporting goods stores. They may also be rented at many signed locations in this area and it's common to see roadside rental stands and even local grocery stores renting the nets for a modest hourly fee. When the run is on, it doesn't take long to build an appetite either. So, what do you do with a bucketful of fresh, squirmy smelt? Check out the selected recipes, tried and true, that may get you hooked on something new.

Beer-Battered Smelt

The flavor is improved by use of milk in the preparation before cooking.

1 to 2 pounds cleaned smelt	1 teaspoon paprika
2 cups milk	1 cup flour, plus flour
1 tablespoon dried oregano	for dusting fish
1 tablespoon seasoned salt	½ cup lemon juice
1 teaspoon seasoned pepper	1 bottle of beer
1 teaspoon garlic salt	

Soak fish in milk for 30 minutes before frying. Mix together oregano, salt, pepper, garlic salt, paprika, flour, and lemon juice. Thin the batter with beer to the consistency of pancake batter. Dust fish with flour, then dip in batter. As batter is used, add more beer to maintain the consistency. This recipe will serve up to four people.

     Note: This batter may also be used for other fish, onion rings, or chicken.

Smoked Smelt

1 to 2 pounds whole smelt	1 tablespoon onion salt
1 cup non-iodized salt	½ teaspoon black pepper
1 cup brown sugar	1 cup soy sauce
1 tablespoon paprika	½ cup cider vinegar
1 tablespoon chili powder	1 tablespoon Worcestershire sauce
1 tablespoon garlic salt	3 cups warm water

Some prefer whole smelt, others remove smelt heads and entrails with a pair of scissors. I simply clip the head off with the scissors and then snip the length of the belly toward the tail and then rinse out the insides. Wash the smelt in clear water. Combine salt, brown sugar, paprika, chili powder, garlic salt, onion salt, black pepper, soy sauce, cider vinegar, Worcestershire sauce, and water.

Let the brine cool and add the smelt. I submerge the fish in the brine and place a heavy plate with a coffee cup on top to weight it down, then I place the brining container in the refrigerator for 8 hours. Rinse the fish thoroughly and let air-dry on paper towels for an hour and smoke the brined smelt until fish surfaces have a dark golden-brown sheen (5 to 7 hours). This recipe easily serves up to four people unless I am the first in line.

44

Visitor-Friendly Hatcheries and Eggs to Fry

*T*he wonderful thing about travel in Oregon is that opportunities to learn more about the Northwest environment are abundant. That's certainly true at this overlooked site that provides varied and interesting environmental lessons about salmon and steelhead at the Oregon Department of Fish and Wildlife's (ODFW) North Nehalem Fish Hatchery in Clatsop County. The site is open daily, no reservations are required, and a visit is absolutely free to the public. Just 90 minutes from Portland, the hatchery offers activities that teach much about the fish and their ties with the aquatic environment. You can see rearing ponds that are brimful of baby salmon or trout, or visit on "spawning day" when you can watch how the next generation of salmon is produced.

In addition, stroll down to the banks of the North Fork of the Nehalem River and check out the unique barrier-free fishing platform where big fish are always on the bite for anglers who need a break. Keep your eyes on the sky as well—bald eagles are known to soar overhead—and closer to ground, Roosevelt elk are often seen in the nearby forests. Make tracks for the Umbrella Falls Trail and enjoy a short, easy, and scenic stroll to reach the namesake falls that offers a stunning moment along the river. It's a place that's never twice the same and will provide lasting memories that may teach you something new about Oregon.

The Oregon Fish and Wildlife Department's Roaring River Hatchery is one of several facilities that raise more than a million catchable trout for stocking at ninety-six lakes and ponds across northwest Oregon. In fact, Roaring River Hatchery's super-large rainbow trout produce so many trout eggs that something special happens to the surplus: they go to school!

Each February, thousands of the surplus trout eggs leave the hatchery and end up in the hands of dedicated volunteers like Leroy Schultz and his friends

Students learn firsthand about the life of trout by raising them in the classroom.

who are members of the not-for-profit sportfishing and conservation group called the Association of Northwest Steelheaders. Schultz passed out packets of eggs to more than a dozen volunteers. Each packet contained 500 eggs wrapped up in a burlap bundle: "Our particular group of the Association of Northwest Steelheaders—the Tualatin Valley Chapter—works with thirty-seven schools to assist with the delivery of eggs and the maintenance of the equipment and the direction of the program," said Shultz. Volunteers like Randy Newton are a critical part of the ODFW education program called Eggs to Fry: "I love giving my time to help because I've got two grandsons that are just nutty about fishing. They're only 6 and 3 years old but this sort of thing connects with them in classrooms and it's the kind of stuff that makes them really excited about fishing too."

The Northwest Steelheaders donate time and raise money to buy expensive equipment to raise the eggs to fry stage. Northwest Steelheaders members Tom VanderPlaat and Kent Reimers also bring enthusiasm to the second graders in Christine McOmie's class at Banks Elementary School. "We do what I call full service," said VanderPlaat. "We bring the tanks into the classrooms; we bring the eggs in as well. We can help facilitate the project from start to finish when the youngsters release the baby fish in a few weeks. We do this all over the state too. It's a really important part of the ODFW and Northwest Steelheaders partnership."

Over the next 6 weeks, the 500 eggs evolve into fish and the experience becomes a launching point of teachable times for writing assignments, science vocabulary, and math lessons in McOmie's class. The students closely monitor the fish each day. They measure water temperature to make sure it's cold enough for fish survival. Even art projects become part of weekly lesson plans that allow kids to explore and express what they've learned about the aquatic environment. "The program takes it from that two-dimensional concept of looking in a book," noted McOmie, "to that three-dimensional piece where the fish are right in front of our eyes—the experience absolutely comes alive."

Former Banks Elementary School Principal Shawnda Sewell agreed the program connects with youngsters in a positive and unique way: "She's able to take this project and make it a thematic unit and cover math, science, and writing and because the kids do have such ownership and engagement with it, the quality of their work definitely shows." Six weeks later, the kids, their parents, and the fish travel together aboard a school bus to a small stream that flows into Henry Hagg Lake in Washington County. "Water's important to all of us and to the fish—especially cold, clean water—this reinforces that message," said VanderPlaat. "By taking care of the fish and releasing them into this stream, it's a lesson and important experience for them."

The Eggs to Fry program recently marked its twentieth anniversary, so thousands of Oregon youngsters have had a chance to learn about aquatic ecology and develop ownership in Oregon's great outdoors. The Oregon Department of Fish and Wildlife offers other programs that many schools can tap into for valuable educational opportunities. Contact the Association of Northwest Steelheaders for more information on how your classroom or school can get involved in the program. Schultz added that even though the young faces change each year, one thing has been a constant from year to year: "The excitement we see in the kids' faces—it's always there. They are so excited to see those fish go in the water and wave good-bye, knowing that they have been successful at a project and that it will be for them in the future."

44 North Nehalem Hatchery

Where: 36751 Fish Hatchery Lane, Nehalem, OR 97131

Web: www.dfw.state.or.us

Phone: 503-368-6828

Association of Northwest Steelheaders

Web: nwsteelheaders.org/conservation/eggs-to-fry

Phone: 503-653-4176

Watch the Episode: www.traveloregon.com/eggstofry

March

45

Higher Wildlife Education

*I*t's funny how some of the best surprises are often found right in your own backyard. So it is from the eastern Cascades point of view where elbow room is measured by the wide-open vistas of snow-shrouded landscapes, the kinds of scenes that capture your heart and may lead you to wonder aloud: "Why have I never traveled this way before?" It is a question on many visitors' minds at a place where the answer is easy to find and higher education is center stage at the High Desert Museum near Bend. You'll agree with the staff's adage that this remarkable complex of displays, demonstrations, and hands-on events makes the museum "more like an expedition than an exhibition."

A great horned owl helps visitors learn about the varied wildlife that live across the high desert.

According to the High Desert Museum's director, Dana Whitelaw, the museum examines and explains the natural history and the special qualities of high desert life: "They may have seen the sign on the highway for years and finally stopped in and people on a regular basis are blown away by how much is here. They experience so much of the West through art, cultural and natural history, and the wildlife. We are proud that we can be that relevant."

From birds of prey, such as hawks and eagles, to river otters and porcupines, this is a place where you can see and learn about the arid Intermountain West, which includes portions of eight western states and the Canadian province of British Columbia. The museum spreads across

You can stroll the grounds and enjoy many trailside exhibits before stepping inside the High Desert Museum to learn more.

150 acres filled with exhibits and demonstrations. A mile-long trail goes through 25 acres of trailside exhibits, including a trout stream, otter ponds, porcupine dens, and historic interpretive displays of frontier life and industry.

A favorite part for me is the Earle A. Chiles Center and a walking tour through vignettes of life called Spirit of the West. This timeline stroll covers thousands of years in the span of a few hundred feet. Along the way, you are invited into a Native American campsite to learn how hardy vegetation, abundant wildlife, and a mineral-rich terrain sustained generations of natives. Then come the explorers and the fur trappers, the miners and sheepherders and sodbusters, and finally the immigrants, fresh off the Oregon Trail. All of this is explained through sights and sounds that put you in the scenes from Stone Age times to rustic dirt roads in a Western frontier town.

Few places convey the story of humans on the desert as well as this experience, including how the mines, then the ranches, and then the railroads brought more and more people to the desert, so that by the 1880s, small cottage industries began to sprout and, in many ways, forever change the face of the desert. A new large-scale exhibit called Sin in the Sagebrush serves up atmosphere and role players in costumes to transport you to Oregon's most recent past. Museum curator Bob Boyd told me that cowhands, buckaroos, trappers, and miners enjoyed a brief escape from the drudgery of daily routines inside the frontier saloon: "For many thousands of people, going west in itself was taking a chance—and if the weather killed your sheep or if your mining claim wasn't paying off—you were a risk taker just showing up. So, perhaps one more turn of the card or spin of that roulette wheel and things might turn around for you."

Other risk takers of the same era included countless homesteaders like Mrs. Blair (portrayed in full costume by local volunteer Linda Evans) who help you to see and understand how tough life was in the high desert as you walk through her replica farmstead from the 1880s. She admitted that the hardest part of all was, "Loneliness, because we're 40 miles from Prineville and it takes 2 days to get there. I go maybe four or five times a year. So we do get lonely. The children keep us busy, but I dearly love to have visitors."

You'll love seeing the many wildlife species on display at the museum too. Hawks, eagles, and turkey vultures are frequently seen soaring over the wide expanse of the desert, but at the museum you can see them all close at hand and learn about their special adaptations for survival. "When it's behind a screen or behind glass, you're so removed," noted wildlife curator Nolan Harvey. "But when you're up close you can see the feathers move, you see the bird move and pay attention to you—that captures your heart and hopefully makes you want to know more about the animal and gives you that bond."

The close connection with wildlife is a lasting legacy message from the museum's founder, Donald Kerr. Kerr owned a passion for wildlife and he was a big believer that animals can connect with newcomers and perhaps change attitudes about the high desert. "We're very proud that all the animals you see here were either captive born or they have been through rehabilitation and cannot be released," added Harvey. "Our wildlife get a second chance at life to educate the rest of us." Whether you're seeking education or recreation, the High Desert Museum will capture your heart and bring you back time and again. "It's a real jewel," noted Whitelaw, "a true treasure of Central Oregon."

---

45 High Desert Museum

Where: 59800 US Highway 97, Bend, OR 97702

Web: www.highdesertmuseum.org

Phone: 541-382-4754

Watch the Episode: www.traveloregon.com/highdesertmuseum

46

Bobber Doggin'
Steelhead

S ome say "March Madness" takes place on the hardwood with a basketball, but fishing guide Josiah Darr said there's another March madness that strikes fishermen who explore Oregon's rivers that wind through the woods. The Nestucca River in Tillamook County is filled with rapids and places where gorgeous sun streams meet the water's rhythm. Darr offered gentle instructions to his two guests, outdoor writer and TV host Gary Lewis and his 17-year-old daughter, Mikayla Lewis. "See the softer water over there on the edge," said Darr. "That is your zone. Cast there!"

The two had traveled from their home in Bend to spend a day fishing for steelhead with Darr—an expert at a fishing technique called "bobber doggin'." Darr uses 10½-foot rods, 30-pound test mainline, a small weight, and a sliding bobber above yarn 'n eggs on a number 2 hook. "This yarn and egg rig is pretty much a standard setup for bobber-doggin' these winter steelhead in big, green water," noted Darr, a young guide who has a passion for fishing. He sported a mile-wide smile and added, "Hopefully the next time we see it, it will be in the corner of a fish's mouth." The technique is to cast the bait and bobber rigging and then float alongside it with the river current. Darr called it a "deadly effective" technique.

"I learned this a few years ago," said Darr. "I just pitch 'em out and away we go. My job is to keep the drift boat at a constant speed and the proper angle so to stay with the bobbers as they drift through a good run of water. You don't catch fish unless your line is in the water, so I keep them out there and stay on them and wait for the next bite." The wait wasn't long as Mikayla's bobber sank without hesitation and she pulled back. She was thrilled when she saw a chrome steelhead shoot through the surface like a rocket.

"Fish on, fish on," yelled Darr. "Easy now—easy. Use the bend of the rod

Guide Josiah Darr said, "A successful day on the river isn't just the catch but the memories that Gary Lewis and his daughter, Mikayla, made for each other."

to fight the fish. Good job, Mikayla!" The 10-pound steelhead was her very first, ever. It was also a wild steelhead, and by regulation, had to go back in the river. Anglers are allowed to keep only hatchery steelhead. Following a 10-minute battle of back and forth, Darr smoothly slid his large net under the gorgeous steelhead and deftly dehooked it and then allowed Mikayla to release it back to the river. "Oh that's wonderful," noted the teen. "My arm was getting tired but he was getting tired too so it all worked out." Darr smiled and added, "That's why I like guiding—moments like this when an angler catches her first. I like it better than reeling them in myself. Good job, Mikayla." It was all of that and more for the teen whose dad began planning their trip nearly 2 years ago. Gary Lewis has fished all over the planet but he said his true love is fishing for steelhead in Oregon.

Soon, his bobber sunk out of sight too. He had his hands full with another gorgeous fish. This one was a hatchery steelhead and a keeper. We could tell it was a hatchery steelhead because the adipose fin was missing—it is a half moon-shaped fin, located just behind the dorsal fin. It was clipped off at the hatchery when the fish was a baby. As Darr slid the net under the fish, he said, "This is our goal—let's do that a lot more. They don't make 'em a whole lot shinier than that. That is a brand-new fresh fish from the ocean: Nestucca River hatchery steelhead." Darr has been guiding on Oregon rivers for several years and his business grew out of a childhood passion for everything outdoors: "It is always awesome being out here—we're right on the Oregon coast in a little river canyon catching these beautiful steelhead. I never feel like I'm going to work, 'cuz I'm doing something I love."

"Every steelhead is a gift," noted Gary. "It's a special thing to accomplish when you catch one too. I like to joke that steelhead are the fish of a thousand casts. Sometimes it feels that way and that makes them all the more special here." "Here" on the river, with its rapids and its steelhead, each angler felt fortunate to be at home—in Oregon. "There's just so much cool stuff to do outdoors in this state," said Darr. "I wouldn't want to live in any other state—I love it here."

Darr advised that conditions can change in a heartbeat at this time of year, so you have to be prepared for the worst and the best that Mother Nature can dish out: from rain, even snow, to brilliant sunshine; anything is possible as winter gives way to spring. So be prepared. The Oregon Department of Fish and Wildlife is a good resource for learning the ropes of steelhead fishing—they even have a website dedicated to teaching you more. You can also visit the Cedar Creek Hatchery to observe the brood stock steelhead and learn more about the Nestucca River program.

46A Cedar Creek Hatchery

Where: 33465 State Highway 22, Hebo, OR 97122
Phone: 503-392-3485

46B JDarr Guided Fishing

Where: 2935 Old Latimer Road, Apt. 1, Tillamook, OR 97141
Web: www.facebook.com/jdarrguidedfishing
Phone: 206-660-1490

Watch the Episode: www.traveloregon.com/driftboatsteelhead

Smith and Bybee
Wetlands Natural Area

*T*here's quite an outdoor show for those in the know at a place where you set your own pace for a walk on the wild side. The Smith and Bybee Wetlands Natural Area is as grass roots as it gets—stroll paths marked with amazing wildlife moments at a time of year brimming with wild critters. It's hard to believe how special a place we have in the Smith and Bybee Wetlands Natural Area. Framed by industrial parks and development on all sides, it is 2,000 acres of cottonwood forest and wetlands, the largest urban lake and marsh in the country. Outdoor writer James Davis recently told me that it's also a premier site for hiking and watching wildlife: "It's big enough—a big, solid chunk not divided up into pieces by roads and such—so it's not fragmented and that's great for wildlife."

While human activity occurs all around, all the time, along an easy paved trail, the city hubbub seemed a million miles away. "It is nature in the city," remarked the exuberant Davis. "Nature in your neighborhood and you don't have to go out to the wilderness to live with wildlife." As Canada geese winged by and a red-tailed hawk soared past on its hunting foray, it was easy to see that waterfowl and raptors provide the best shows that you can watch in winter. "It is pretty unbelievable to most people," added

You can duck in and out of foul winter weather at the Smith and Bybee Wetlands wildlife viewing station.

Davis. "We have two pairs of bald eagles nesting here, we've got a nesting colony of great blue herons, we've even had tundra swans hanging out here in the winter. Really, any bird that comes through the Portland area can show up here." But what doesn't show up much are people. I wondered aloud, "Could Smith and Bybee Wetlands be a well-kept secret?" "Perhaps," nodded Davis.

Although as Metro's point man of sorts and the park's naturalist for the past dozen years, he insisted that the word is getting out and more folks are discovering the many pleasures that the wetlands offered—either on the easy hiking trail or in a canoe with a paddle. In fact, Davis does all he can to spread the word about Smith and Bybee Wetlands, and other local places too, through his book *The Northwest Nature Guide*, a month-by-month, comprehensive wildlife watching guide with 75 color photos and extensive maps and directions. Top of his local list for newcomers: Crystal Springs Rhododendron Garden in southeast Portland. "It is the best beginner's bird-watching place in Portland," exclaimed Davis. "I've been there on a bird walk in February and we saw thirteen different species of waterfowl without binoculars. There may not be a lot there, but the diversity is just spectacular."

Fast on the wings of Crystal Springs comes the relatively new Tualatin River National Wildlife Refuge in Sherwood: "Ah, they really planned the trail across the refuge right," said Davis. "It's in such an excellent location so that you can get out there, see them, and yet there are many other areas closed to the public. So, the birds actually have a refuge on the refuge." Part of the wonder of Smith and Bybee Wetlands Natural Area is that it's not on the way to anywhere; you must go there to explore it for yourself on a journey of discovery. Davis explained: "It's one of the things that makes Portland such a great place to live. The idea is that nature doesn't have to be way away from people. We can have nature in the city, nature in the neighborhoods; we can have urban wildlife."

---

47 Smith and Bybee Wetlands Natural Area

Where: 5300 North Marine Drive, Portland, OR 97203

Phone: 503-797-1850

Watch the Episode: www.traveloregon.com/smithbybee

Wild in the City

*T*ime in the outdoors can refresh the eye and lift the spirit and the beauty of Oregon is that you won't travel far to find it. *Wild in the City: Exploring the Intertwine* was copublished by the Portland Audubon Society and Oregon State University Press. Mike Houck and M. J. Cody coedited and wrote essays for the impressive collection of writings and practical nature-finding "ramblings." "The book is really educational for people who enjoy our parks," noted Cody. "But if they lack a sense for the Northwest—that lifelong depth—that's what we also provide in the book."

More than 100 writers contributed to finding the "wild in the city"; authors who wrote the text, prepared the maps, sketched wildlife drawings, and really provided the nuts and bolts of locating the Portland area's parks, trails, and refuges. From Washington County's Fernhill Wetlands where flocks of geese fill the sky to the region's eastern edge at Oxbow Park on the Sandy River that seems more wilderness than campground. There are also well-known wildlife areas, like Sauvie Island, that continue to fill us with wonder and surprise, noted the Audubon Society's Bob Sallinger, a dedicated naturalist who enjoyed one particular essay: "A piece called 'Raptor Road Trip' is all about the different places you can visit on the island—whether you hike, bike, or drive or paddle. It's simply phenomenal wildlife viewing and winter is really a spectacular time of year to get out and see wildlife." Whether you are a longtime resident, a newcomer, or just passing through Portland, you will fall in love with *Wild in the City.*

It's far more than a guidebook for the text also presents a call to action and a new way to look at the expanding network of connections between the wild places that we prize: a network that is called the Intertwine. "The Intertwine is a name for the region's network of trails, parks, and natural areas," noted Metro's Dan Moeller. Moeller is Metro's natural areas land manager, the agency that manages much of the 14,000-

plus acres of parks, trails, and natural areas acquired through two voter-approved bond measures. "You can find everything from beautiful wetlands to oak woodlands to prairies and upland forests," added Moeller. "You can find a little bit of everything and it is really magnificent land."

The Intertwine is growing all of the time too. In fact, recent additions include Cooper Mountain Nature Park near Beaverton, Graham Oaks Nature Park near Wilsonville, and Mount Talbert Nature Park in Clackamas County. Each site is distinct, each offers special features, and each is connected as natural space and outdoor environmental classroom. "That's exactly what the Intertwine is," said Moeller. "It goes beyond bureaucracies and boundaries and it works among varied agencies, communities, and cities to bring all of these parks and natural spaces together. Citizens can go out and enjoy them as seamlessly and easily as possible."

The Intertwine

Where: 2100 SW River Parkway, Suite 450, Portland, OR 97201

Web: www.theintertwine.org

Phone: 503-445-0991

Watch the Episode: www.traveloregon.com/intertwine

The Last Wild Run

On the surface it may sound like some sort of curious crazy race, but "the last wild run" has nothing to do with one athlete versus another. Although the last wild run is in the middle of nowhere and you work up a sweat to reach it, it isn't an Olympic event, but it feels that way in steep, rocky country where one misstep or a slip could really cost you. There are no major roadways, highways, or even a gentle country road to reach the last wild run. It's inaccessible to the extreme. So, consider Ian Fergusson, a Salmonberry River Steward, something of a long-distance champion at what has does—each week for 3 months—and he has done it for each of the last 20 spring seasons: "From the landslides you have to climb over and the road washouts you must dodge, it's not an easy stroll by any means," noted Fergusson. He hikes up to 15 miles a day, peers into the North Fork of the Salmonberry River, and keeps tabs on something truly special for the Oregon Department of Fish and Wildlife (ODFW) in the remote Salmonberry River Basin, the last wild run of steelhead that live in a remote Oregon river.

The North Fork of the Salmonberry is a river full of foamy falls and the fish must jump one particular waterfall to survive. It is the only way they can reach the safe and smooth upriver water to spawn. We can count their successes—one after the other as the river roars through the 10-foot-high cleft in the ancient basalt rock. It is a heart-pounding moment when the wild steelhead are swimming and jumping over and over. "These are wild steelhead and what they do is really an athletic event; it's just an amazing spectacle to watch these fish jump one after the other," noted Fergusson. Steelhead are often called the "street fighters" of the salmon world because they have to swim to the farthest, highest ends of the watershed and endure the toughest conditions that Mother Nature serves up.

"I just love this system and these fish," said Fergusson with a beaming smile. "These fish are just so special to me. I used to fish the Salmonberry River a lot, but I don't even do that anymore. I just come here to watch and count these fish."

It is remarkable that the fish are even there. The Salmonberry River Canyon is gigantic, but it was destroyed when the Tillamook Burn devastated the canyon forest beginning 80 years ago. "Years and years of erosion and silt washing into the river," noted Fergusson, "no cover on the stream banks, much of it burned off and yet these fish managed to hold on during that period." The fish not only held on, they thrived. More impressive is the fact that there's never been a hatchery on the river, so the last wild run of Salmonberry steelhead are truly rare. You can count on one hand the number of Oregon streams that have them. These days, the fish are protected by rules that allow catch and release angling in the main stem, but prohibits all angling in the tributaries.

Fergusson not only counts the fish that jump for survival, but he counts the "redds" or nests that the female steelhead gouge out of the gravel with their tails. "It's a light colored area—much lighter than the surrounding substrate and the eggs are buried right there," he added. Still, for all its remoteness, logging is nearby and clear-cuts are closing in on canyon walls. That activity worries Fergusson and gives him even more motivation to collect data for the state's fish agency that hasn't the regular manpower to dedicate to such a distant river. "We really count on volunteers like Ian," said Chris Knutsen, the ODFW district fish biologist. "He and his friends come in here regularly and help by telling us what's going on in the watershed. He has a good handle on the biology, the ecology of north coast watersheds, and he has a lot of valuable information to share. Clearly, he's demonstrating that he cares about the resource."

"I guess it's because I wanted to help do something with the management of the resource," noted Fergusson. "These fish are very resilient and they have endured for many, many years and we hope that they can keep doing it. If we do all we can to protect the places that are special, then maybe they can hang on." The volunteer fish counters want to make sure the Salmonberry River remains one of those streams. "This is what I really love to do," added Fergusson. "This, to me, is recreation. I come out here all day, slogging around in streams and counting fish, counting their redds, and then I hike up here and watch this waterfall jumping. It's recreation for me and it's astounding." For more information on how to volunteer on the Salmonberry River Steelhead project you can contact the Association of Northwest Steelheaders (see page 185), Trout Unlimited (see page 69), or the Native Fish Society.

48 Salmonberry River

Where: An approximately 20-mile-long tributary of the Nehalem River in the
Tillamook State Forest. It rises in northeastern Tillamook County and
flows west-northwest through the Coast Range Mountains, joining the
Nehalem River from the southeast about 15 miles northeast of the
city of Nehalem.

Native Fish Society

Where: 221 Molalla Avenue, Suite 100, Oregon City, OR 97045

Web: nativefishsociety.org

Phone: 503-496-0807

Oregon Department of Fish and Wildlife Salmon and Trout Enhancement Program (STEP)

Web: www.dfw.state.or.us/fish/step

Phone: 503-947-6232 or 503-842-2741

Watch the Episode: www.traveloregon.com/lastwildrun

Index